gestalten

The MONOCLE
Travel Guide Series

10

Paris

For more information, please visit *gestalten.com*

Bibliographic information published by the Deutsche Nationalbibliothek: The Deutsche Nationalbibliothek lists this publication in the Deutsche Nationalbibliografie; detailed bibliographic data are available online at *dnb.d-nb.de*

MIX
Paper from responsible sources
FSC www.fsc.org FSC® C011712

This book was printed on paper certified by the FSC®

Monocle editor in chief: *Tyler Brûlé*
Monocle editor: *Andrew Tuck*
Series editor: *Joe Pickard*
Guide editor: *Amy Richardson*

Designed by *Monocle*
Proofreading by *Monocle*
Typeset in *Plantin & Helvetica*

Printed by *Offsetdruckerei Grammlich, Pliezhausen*

Made in Germany

Published by *Gestalten*, Berlin 2016
ISBN 978-3-89955-658-2

2nd printing, 2017

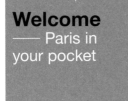

Welcome
Paris in your pocket

Ah, *Paris*. There are few cities in the world that evoke the same level of sentiment: it's the *City of Light*, the City of Love, Gay Paree. The iconography runs deep: baguettes; paint palettes; *breton shirts* and *berets*; supercilious waiters in white aprons; chic Parisiennes with small dogs.

This guide, however, seeks to cut through the clichés and steer you away from the tourist-thronged sites to discover the "real" Paris. That's not to say we don't pay dues to its rich history and cultural heritage; any visit should include time exploring the myriad museums and galleries. But we gently suggest forsaking the Musée du Louvre and opting for those lesser-known: a fashion exhibition perhaps, to pay homage to the city's *couture luminaries*, or sculptor Rodin's revamped former home to wander among the masterpieces in the garden.

MONOCLE's team of editors and on-the-ground reporters have cherrypicked their favourite places, from the smartest hotels to the *liveliest winebars* and the best restaurants. The retail chapter will help you fine-tune your method for tackling the city's overwhelming number of fashion and luxury-goods retailers.

Whether it's sourcing a chic champagne bar to sample *Normandy oysters*, whiling away the hours people-watching in Jean-Paul Sartre's favourite bistro or exploring the archives of *modernist master Le Corbusier*, this guide will expose you to what we consider the most winsome of Paris's innumerable charms. *Bon voyage.* — (M)

Contents
Navigating the city

Use the key below to help navigate the guide section by section.

- **H** Hotels
- **F** Food and drink
- **R** Retail
- **T** Things we'd buy
- **E** Essays
- **C** Culture
- **D** Design and architecture
- **S** Sport and fitness
- **W** Walks

Map
— The city at a glance

Paris is one of the great world cities and the scale and variety of its charms can be daunting. Where to begin? In fact navigating the French capital is quite straightforward, with the city divided into 20 arrondissements. Starting with the 1st in the centre, these administrative districts (often known by Roman numerals) form a snail-shaped spiral. The names of Metro stations are also useful shorthand for specific areas. And of course the city is divided by the Seine: to the south of the river is the Left Bank (historically associated with the city's intellectual life), to the north the Right Bank.

But these terms aren't just geographical markers but areas with their own distinctive flavour. From the plush elegance of the 16th to the bobo vitality of the 10th, each arrondissement offers its own experience. This is a city that has inexhaustible sights and secret spots to discover – let us show you our favourites.

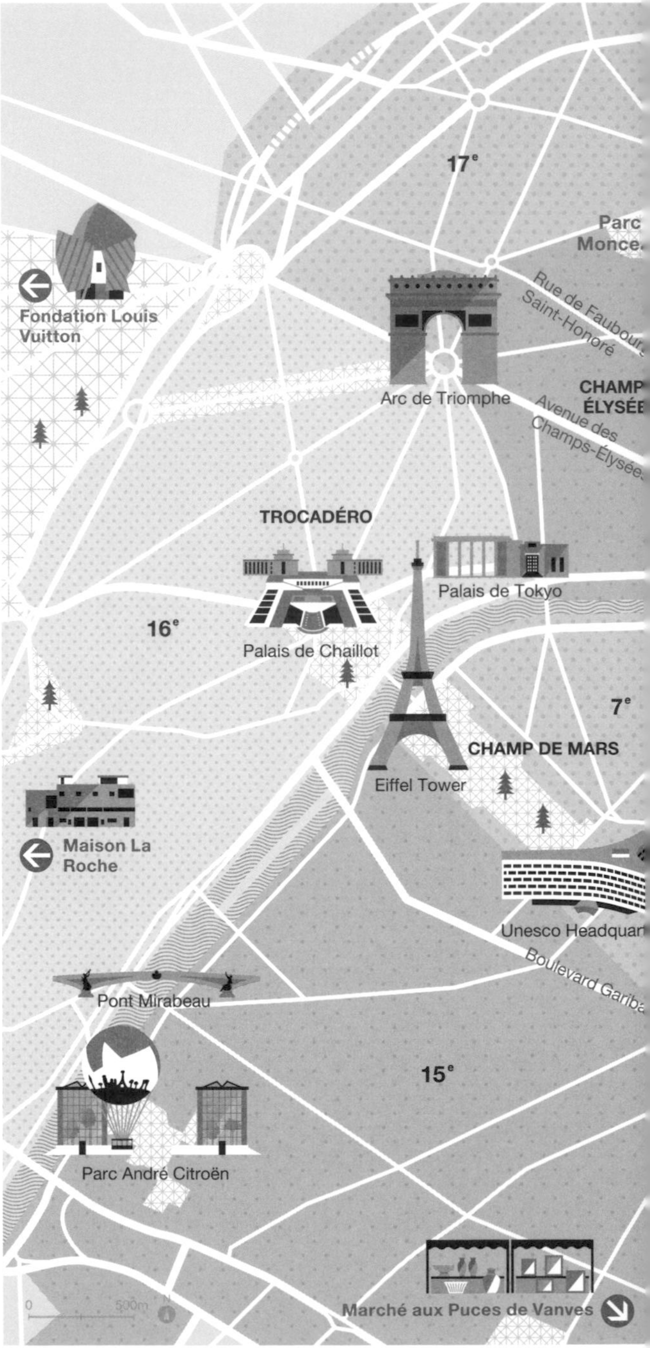

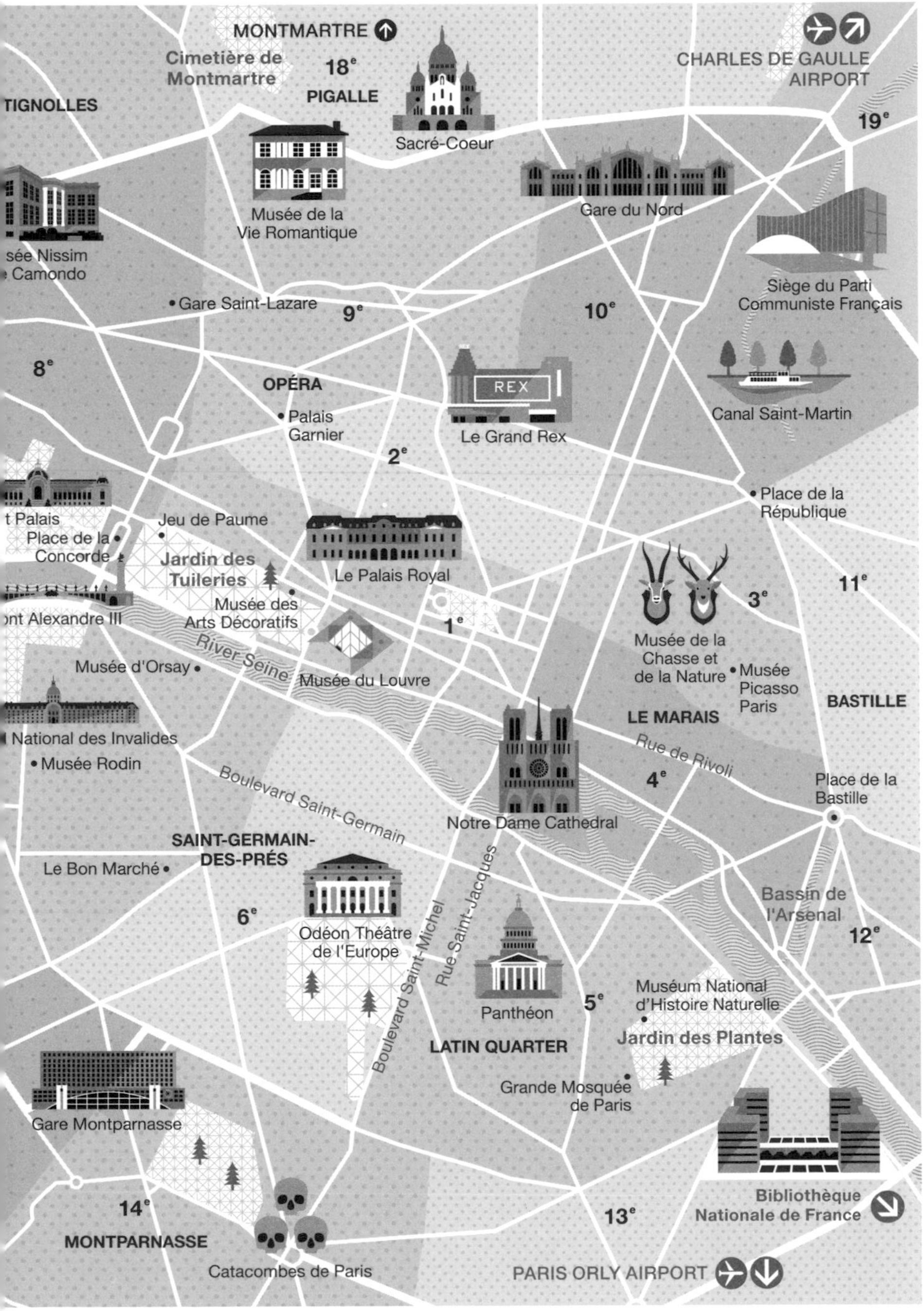
MONTMARTRE
Cimetière de Montmartre
18e
PIGALLE
Sacré-Coeur
TIGNOLLES
CHARLES DE GAULLE AIRPORT
19e
Musée de la Vie Romantique
Gare du Nord
sée Nissim
Camondo
Siège du Parti Communiste Français
Gare Saint-Lazare
9e
10e
8e
OPÉRA
REX
Le Grand Rex
Canal Saint-Martin
Palais Garnier
2e
Place de la République
t Palais
Place de la Concorde
Jeu de Paume
Jardin des Tuileries
Le Palais Royal
Musée des Arts Décoratifs
1e
3e
11e
ont Alexandre III
River Seine
Musée d'Orsay
Musée du Louvre
Musée de la Chasse et de la Nature
Musée Picasso Paris
BASTILLE
LE MARAIS
National des Invalides
Musée Rodin
Rue de Rivoli
4e
Place de la Bastille
Boulevard Saint-Germain
Notre Dame Cathedral
SAINT-GERMAIN-DES-PRÉS
Le Bon Marché
Rue Saint-Jacques
Bassin de l'Arsenal
6e
Odéon Théâtre de l'Europe
Boulevard Saint-Michel
12e
Muséum National d'Histoire Naturelle
Panthéon
5e
LATIN QUARTER
Jardin des Plantes
Grande Mosquée de Paris
Gare Montparnasse
Bibliothèque Nationale de France
14e
13e
MONTPARNASSE
Catacombes de Paris
PARIS ORLY AIRPORT

Need to know

Get to grips with the basics

How to drink (a lot) and kiss (even more) like a Parisian, navigate the city with aplomb and avoid being caught out by idiosyncratic opening hours. Read on for some quick facts and helpful tips when visiting Paris.

First impressions
Etiquette

Despite their brusque reputation, manners matter to Parisians. Always preface any new conversation with a "Bonjour madame/monsieur". Whether you're asking for a croissant or directions, don't just launch straight into your request: it's considered wildly impolite. Even if your French is terrible (or non-existent), a pleasantry is a key element to a smooth exchange.

Kiss kiss
Greetings

The double air-kiss (*la bise*) on both cheeks is a given in any social context in France. Both men and women take part in the practice whether they're old friends or new acquaintances. So if you're meeting up with a group, get ready to pucker up (French people from certain regions outside Paris may even spring a third kiss on you). In a professional context, a simple nod or a handshake usually does the trick. French people do not hug each other.

I'm ready to become a kissing soldier

Navigating the city
Neighbourhoods

There are 20 districts (arrondissements) that make up central Paris. Although the numbering system may seem frustratingly arbitrary at first, it follows a clockwise swirl with Louvre in the 1st arrondissement at the centre. The arrondissement is indicated by the last two digits of Parisian postal codes (75001-75020) and displayed at the top of street signs. For ease of use, we've listed the arrondissement after each venue name in this guide.

The naming of the various *banlieues* (suburbs) can also confuse first-time visitors; Parisians may refer to specific areas according to the closest monument (Bastille, Louvre) or Metro station (Opéra, Oberkampf). You'll find the major districts outlined on our map (*see page 12*) but keep in mind that smaller unofficial neighbourhoods, such as the Latin Quarter, sit within these and are more fuzzily defined.

Banking on it
The east/west divide

Paris's Left and Right banks are not simply demarcated by geography: they represent different lifestyles. While the Left Bank (south of the Seine) was the bohemian hub of the early 20th century – where writers and artists lived hedonistically in decadence or squalor – today it's a swathe of art galleries, upscale cafés and chic residences. The Right Bank is more varied: its west is elegant and expensive; the east hip and youthful; the north a mix of touristy, ethnic and charming.

In vino veritas
Drinking

Wine is the tipple of choice in Paris (and in many bars and restaurants, it's cheaper than a soft drink). It pays to have some French adjectives in your pocket to indicate your preferences – *sucré* (sweet), *sec* (dry), *énorme* (huge – well, you are here to have fun), etc – so you can communicate with your waiter effectively.

The craze for "natural wines" – made with no chemicals and minimal intervention from standard cellar practices – is in full swing here. Craft beers are a little harder to find; it's still a fledgling industry.

French people are also partial to meeting for an *apéro* (a drink and a bite to eat, usually a cheese and charcuterie platter) between the hours of 18.00 and 20.00.

One more glass of Parisian courage and I'll tackle the – hic! – steps

Do your homework
Opening hours

It can't be emphasised enough: always look online or call ahead to check that the venue you want to visit is open. Many an intrepid traveller has been caught out by an unexpectedly shuttered museum or restaurant. Cultural institutions are typically closed on Mondays but some also bar their doors on Tuesdays (and some, annoyingly, do both).

Parisian restaurants have no synchronicity: most open only five or six days a week but figuring out *which* do *when* is the rub. Some shut on the weekends or Monday to Tuesday; others only offer lunch on weekdays. Don't waste your time looking for the logic, it will drive you mad.

Also keep in mind that in many traditional restaurants, meals are served at relatively rigid times: lunch is usually from 12.30 to 14.00 while dinner runs from 20.00 to 22.30. If you show up outside these hours you risk being turned away hungry (or at least in search of a kebab or crêpe). Newer venues tend to be more flexible with their service times.

Building a city
Urban layout

In the 18th century, Paris was a far cry from the boulevard-lined beauty that we enjoy strolling around today. Poor sanitation, overcrowding and a haphazard layout meant that disease was rife and the roads traffic-congested. Napoleon III commissioned Baron Georges-Eugène Haussmann to conduct a full-scale rip-out and revamp of streets, parks and buildings. Kilometres of wide boulevards were cut to create fluid routes and organise the city into arrondissements (*see opposite*). New buildings were required to conform to strict height and style guidelines, resulting in Paris's distinctive cityscape with its cream façades and zinc roofing.

It's August, so I'm making like the locals and flying south

Summer escape
Holiday periods

If New York is the city that never sleeps, Paris is the city that's always on holiday. Parisians value lifestyle and rest and take frequent time off to make sure they get enough of both. During the summer months, restaurants, cafés and shops can be closed for weeks. If you're in the city between July and September, be sure to check opening hours. Chances are, staff are taking siestas in Italy or the south of France. National holidays and school breaks can also interrupt service.

Pick of the bunch
Keep your belongings safe

Paris's pickpockets are predatory with tourists. Be particularly wary of young children bearing clipboards: it's a distraction technique so that a hand can be slipped into your pocket. When entering Metro stations be aware of people attempting to sneak in the turnstile with you and always keep your bags zipped. It also pays to be discreet when using your phone because the grab-and-go tactic is an unfortunately regular occurrence.

Hotels
—— Suite Française

Paris loves its grand old storied hotels so much it has a special status for those that surpass French standards of excellence: the Palace distinction. You'll find three such lavish institutions here – Le Bristol, Park Hyatt and the Four Seasons Hotel George V – but we've also looked beyond the big players to find places that emphasise hospitality and personality regardless of their room count.

From design-oriented boltholes to wildly wall-papered guesthouses, the city's boutique hotels are dynamic and characterful. We dish out points for the odd quirk too, whether it's a tape recorder in the wall at Hôtel Particulier Montmartre (to leave a message for the next occupants) or Hôtel Grand Amour's anatomically inspired carpets.

But what all of these places have in common is their understanding of the importance of exceptional service, thoughtful design and a welcoming spot in which to socialise at the end of the day – whether that's a lively bar or a peaceful courtyard.

Here are our favourite places to hang our *chapeau* while in town.

High light
A 1960s lamp is the centrepiece of the salon

①
Hôtel Henriette, Croulebarbe (13e)
Romantic bohemia

Former fashion stylist and interior designer Vanessa Scoffier is the creative spirit behind the refurbishment of this intimate hotel in Paris's up-and-coming 13th arrondissement. The 32 bedrooms and communal spaces are filled with vintage furniture – much of it Scandinavian – sourced by Scoffier from flea markets in Paris and abroad. Textured natural materials such as vintage pressed-tin panels and rope light fixtures playfully combine with patterned wallpapers and pops of bright paintwork. "The overall idea was to make it like a family home," says Scoffier. "I hadn't planned anything. It was all about feeling."

The courtyard is a lovely place to sit with a coffee in the sun and breakfast is served each morning in the communal canteen. Expect a warm welcome, fresh flowers in your room and a croissant on your plate in the morning.

9 Rue des Gobelins, 75013
+33 (0)1 4707 2690
hotelhenriette.com

MONOCLE COMMENT: Staff pride themselves on helping guests to experience the city "like real Parisians" and will assist you to build an itinerary for your stay.

2

Hôtel Grand Amour,
Gare du Nord (10e)
Arty lodgings with spice

This 42-room guesthouse was opened in 2015 by hip trio Thierry Costes, Emmanuel Delavenne and André Saraiva, combining the charm of a B&B with grand-hotel luxury. "It redefines what the industry is about: it's more generous and more fun," says Delavenne.

Graffiti artist Saraiva (*pictured, on right, with Delavenne*) styled the interiors. The walls bear artworks by the likes of Helmut Newton and Keith Haring, bathrooms are kitted out with Hermès toiletries and the staff uniforms were designed by Maison Kitsuné. You won't find a television – but why would you want to when you can socialise over a glass of wine in the courtyard or the bar?
18 Rue de la Fidélité, 75010
+33 (0)1 4416 0330
hotelamourparis.fr/grandamour

MONOCLE COMMENT: Keep an eye out for the genitalia-patterned carpet custom-designed by Saraiva.

New neighbours

Bastille's newest hotel, Maison Breguet, is a 53-room boutique affair with plenty of nostalgic, 1960s chic. Restaurateur David Lanher is behind the in-house bistro, while the music, artwork and library come courtesy of Parisian artists.
maisonbreguet.com

3
Park Hyatt, Place Vendôme (2e)
Modern classic

This hotel at one of the city's most illustrious addresses, Place Vendôme, only opened its doors in 2002 but it already possesses a timeless air. US designer Ed Tuttle was asked to reference major French style trends when creating the interiors and accordingly it bears everything from art deco elements to the grand decorative flourishes of Louis XVI.

The 153-room hotel has a host of 200 sq m presidential suites (that naturally have every bell and whistle you could dream of) but even the junior suites here are excellent. For dining there's the Michelin-starred Pur' restaurant (chef Jean-François Rouquette offers both à la carte and two tasting menus) and two bars, where malt whiskies and champagnes are particularly well represented. The hotel also creates its own signature scent and has partnered with a distillery to make gin – which gives you some sense of the level of attention to detail you'll find here.
5 Rue de la Paix, 75002
+33 (0)1 5871 1234
hyatt.com

MONOCLE COMMENT: All the big players in fashion and luxury goods have shops around Place Vendôme so it's a good base for serious shoppers.

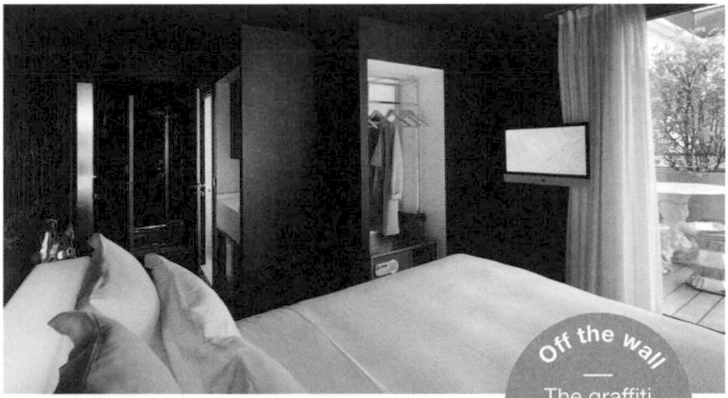

Off the wall

The graffiti tells the history of the hotel

4

Mama Shelter, Pére-Lachaise (20e)
Party hotel with style

This fun hotel was founded by Jeremie Trigano and his family in 2008 to fill a hole they saw in the market. "We wanted to create a destination rather than just rooms – to reinvent the affordable hotel," Trigano says.

They went about this by ditching fripperies such as bathrobes and superfluous decoration and concentrating on the essentials: the 172 rooms boast luxurious beds, free movies, iMacs and quality skincare products. Philippe Starck designed the playful interiors.

Thursday to Saturdays, DJs and bands make this one of the hottest venues in town; Justin Timberlake, Jay Z and Beyoncé have all come here to party.
109 Rue de Bagnolet, 75020
+33 (0)1 4348 4848
mamashelter.com

MONOCLE COMMENT: The gourmet all-you-can-eat buffet on Sundays will aid your post-party recovery.

I've got everything I need – apart from my taxi fare

5

Le Pigalle, Pigalle (9e)
Neighbourhood snapshot

This 40-room hotel is a collaborative concept that brings together the neighbourhood's best offerings – "A portal to Pigalle," says owner Valéry Grégo. The croissants are fresh from the local *boulangerie*; the wine is from the slopes of Montmartre; the flowers are sourced from the neighbourhood *fleurier*. Even the marble flooring was the type fashionable in 19th-century Pigalle.

With food available at the bar and restaurant, live music on Friday nights and a cocktail lounge (don't miss barwoman Gwladys Gublin's spicy speciality, the Pauvre Chérie), Le Pigalle is a magnet for travellers looking for a good time and a hotel with some flair.
9 Rue Frochot, 75009
+33 (0)1 4878 3714
lepigalle.paris

MONOCLE COMMENT: A nice touch in every room is the record-player and 15 vinyl delights handpicked by Pigalle DJ Victor Kiswell.

⑥
Le Bristol, Madeleine (8e)
Tradition with a twist

This Parisian institution first opened its doors in 1925 and has been in the hands of the Oetker family since 1978. Situated on the gallery-lined Rue du Faubourg Saint-Honoré, steps from the Élysée Palace, Le Bristol offers the old-school etiquette and service Paris is known for. The grand lobby and its 188 rooms and suites are decorated with Louis XV and XVI style furnishings. Keep an eye out for pampered hotel feline Fa-Raon, who enjoys napping in the foyer armchairs.

Three-Michelin-starred chef Éric Frechon helms up the fine-dining restaurant Epicure. In the evenings Le Bar du Bristol buzzes with guests enjoying head barman Maxime Hoerth's signature Bristol Old Fashioned No.1 (made with a swish of bourbon and roasted coffee beans).
112 Rue du Faubourg, 75008
+33 (0)1 5343 4300
lebristolparis.com

MONOCLE COMMENT: It's hard to beat the hotel's sixth-floor pool, designed by architect Caesar Pinnau. It's built to resemble the deck of a luxurious sailing boat from the 1920s and large windows look out over the Eiffel Tower to the west and Sacré-Coeur to the east.

7

The Hoxton, Bonne Nouvelle (2^{e})
Regal refit

It's a shame that not all of the down-at-heel buildings in Paris are as sensitively restored as the Hoxton in the 2nd. Opened in mid-2017, the five-storey space dates back to the 18th century, when it was built for an adviser to Louis XV, and comes complete with two cobbled courtyards decked out with smart Roda chairs and Tuuci umbrellas.

The suave 400-cover Rivié restaurant and Jacques' Bar are great places from which to watch the capital's cooler customers convene, while the airy lobby sees as many dapper walk-throughs as the average Parisian catwalk. There are 172 rooms but no suites – in keeping with the brand's ethos of charging a fair price for the night – and there's been no skimping on the looks (think reclaimed herringbone parquet floors, cornicing and wall panelling) thanks to Parisian firm Humbert & Poyet.
30-32 Rue du Sentier, 75002
+33 (0)1 8565 7500
thehoxton.com

MONOCLE COMMENT: The outdoor courtyard may be appealing but inside is just as lush, with green walls by landscapers Jardin de Gally that brim with pothos, maranta plants and split-leaf philodendra.

(8)
Four Seasons Hotel George V Paris, Champs-Élysées (8e)
High-end luxury

Located a few short blocks from Avenue des Champs-Élysées, this hotel stays faithful to its grand address. While under the stewardship of François Dupré from 1928 to 1968, the hotel built up an impressive collection of 18th-century furniture and artwork and now this is a hallmark of the establishment. One such piece – Nicolas Poussin's "Landscape with Diogenes" – greets guests in the reception.

True to the Four Seasons experience, all 244 rooms are designed for comfort and many have private terraces. In addition to an excellent concierge service, the hotel offers two restaurants (Le Cinq has a Michelin star), two bars, a wine cellar and a spa and fitness centre.
31 Avenue George V, 75008
+33 (0)1 4952 7000
fourseasons.com

MONOCLE COMMENT: Designer Pierre-Yves Rochon was given carte blanche to create the hotel's apartment-sized Penthouse Suite. It comes complete with six terraces, one of which has a private dining area. Enjoy a night cap while taking in a 360-degree view over the Paris rooftops.

Get an Eiffel
—
Many of the rooms have private terraces

Hotel bars

01 **Bar Hemingway at Ritz Hotel, Place Vendôme:** The city's most renowned hotel bar is as famous for its head barman as its namesake. Colin Field has been shaking up the house speciality, the calvados-based "Serendipity" cocktail, since 1994.
ritzparis.com

02 **Café Laurent at Hotel d'Aubusson, Saint-Germain-des-Prés:** This has been a favoured haunt for literary and jazz figures since the 17th century; Voltaire, Camus and Sartre have all bent an elbow here. The piano bar and luxurious salon remain popular with the area's chic residents. Sit back and relax in front of the fireplace with the signature cocktail "Laurent".
hoteldaubusson.com

03 **Bar 228 at Le Meurice, Tuileries:** It may have been redesigned by Philippe Starck in 2007 but the century-old Bar 228 has retained its timeless charm. Head barman William Oliveri's Bellini has enthralled the likes of Sofia Loren and Elizabeth Taylor since 1987 and the "croque Meurice" is the epitome of tasty comfort food.
lemeurice.com

Ritzy overhaul

The 118-year-old Ritz Paris has undergone a €200m refurbishment overseen by architect Thierry Despont. From Bar Hemingway to the top-floor suites, not only was the whole place spruced up but it also opened the world's first Chanel spa, a Turkish bath and a swimming pool.

9

Hôtel Particulier Montmartre, Montmartre (18e)
Quirky glamour

This plush boutique hotel belonged to the Guerrand-Hermès family before being transformed into accommodation by Morgane Rousseau in 2007. The decor of the five suites is strikingly individual and each was conceived by a different contemporary artist.

The hotel is now overseen by Rousseau's 27-year-old son Oscar Comtet. He has added to the homespun touches by introducing chickens for fresh eggs and black bees for honey; both appear on the dinner menu available to guests from Wednesdays to Saturdays, and brunch throughout the weekend.

Most recently, Comtet opened Le Très Particulier cocktail bar in the basement. We recommend enjoying a L'Attrape-Coeurs or Le Malaparte cocktail (or perhaps both) as an *apéro* in the pretty garden designed by architect Louis Bénech.
23 Avenue Junot, 75018
+33 (0)1 5341 8140
hotel-particulier-montmartre.com

MONOCLE COMMENT: In a playful (if somewhat bizarre) touch, the Trees With Ears suite has a tape-recorder embedded in the wall so that you can leave a message for the next guests.

Those Le Malaparte cocktails really pack a punch

(10)

Hôtel Providence, République (10e)
Boutique charisma

There is a dearth of four-star hotels in Paris's east. Happily, Hôtel Providence has emerged. Owners Pierre and Elodie Moussié trawled through flea markets for more than a year to deck out their 18-room hotel, bar and restaurant: the result is eclectic and charming. The vibrant foliage-and-floral-pattern wallpapers by House of Hackney and Madeleine Castaing add a lush, decadent air.

Every detail has been considered, from the USB socket above each bedside table to the personal bar in every room (which comes with utensils, ice cubes and cocktail instructions). The brasserie has a pretty terrace and serves delicious dishes from the wood-fired oven.
90 Rue René Boulanger, 75010
+33 (0)1 4634 3404
hotelprovidenceparis.com

MONOCLE COMMENT: There are numerous theatres nearby so actors come here for post-show drinks, making for a colourful crowd.

I think I fit in quite well with this arty crowd

Paris hotspot

The hotel is close to Canal Saint-Martin

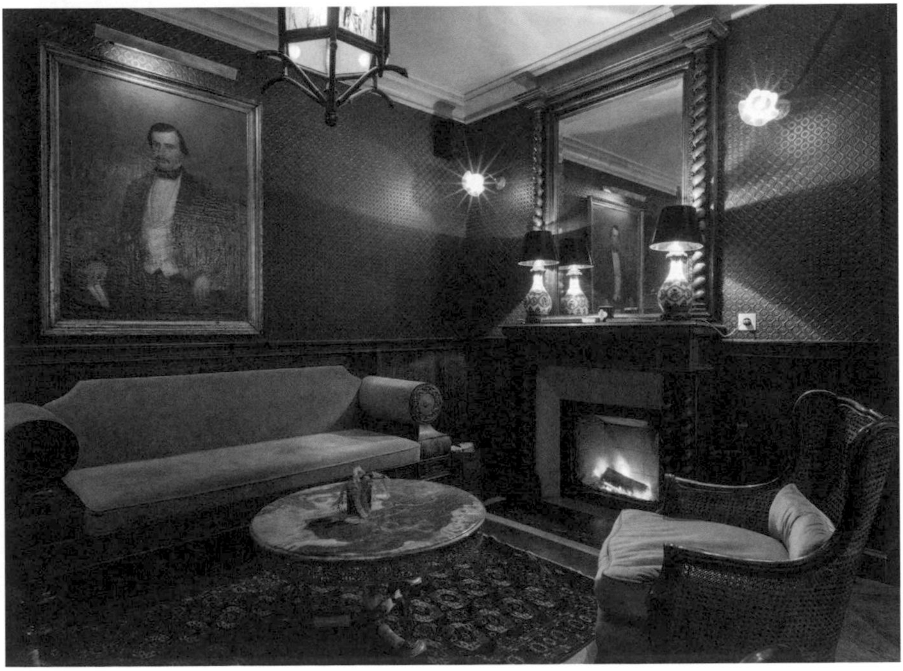

⑪
Hôtel Daniel, Champs-Élysées (8e)
Chinoiserie charm

Tucked off the Champs-Élysées is this sister hotel to the Albergo in Beirut. And like its sibling, what we like is that it does its own thing; this is no identikit hotel. Mixing Lebanese, French and Chinese twists (to name a few), designer Tarfa Salam has created a colourful and exotic bolthole. There are 26 rooms, seven of which are suites. The restaurant is very good and the staff know that manners matter.
8 Rue Frédéric Bastiat, 75008
+33 (0)1 4256 1700
hoteldanielparis.com

MONOCLE COMMENT: Afternoon tea is an event here, with loose-leaf varieties by French brand Mariage Frères.

⑫
Hôtel du Temps, Poissonnière (9e)
Simple city escape

Yoan Marciano's 2013-established hotel near the leafy Square Montholon offers a quintessentially Parisian sanctuary. The decor, designed by Alix Thomsen and Laura Léonard, features comfy vintage furniture paired with paintings by artist Rafael Alterio. The 23 airy bedrooms are low-key but comfortably kitted out with luxurious bedding and skincare products by Swedish brand L:A Bruket.

We recommend taking a seat at the custom-made redwood bar and ordering a "Cocktail du Temps": a concoction of Japanese whisky, lime, ginger, mint and spices.

"We wanted to create a retreat for visitors and Parisians alike," says Marciano. "Parisians like to escape the city and when they do, they stay here."
11 Rue de Montholon, 75009
+33 (0)1 4770 3716
hotel-du-temps.fr

MONOCLE COMMENT: Marciano likes to greet his guests personally over a coffee or a walk around the neighbourhood, which he compares to east London's Shoreditch. Our pick of the rooms is room 601, the well-appointed top-floor suite.

⑬
The Peninsula, Trocadéro (16e)
Heritage wonder

The Peninsula Paris is the venerable Hong Kong-based hotelier's first foray into European territory. Inside the elegant 200-room venture – just a stone's throw from the Champs-Élysées – you'll find a spa with a gym and a swimming pool, plus six restaurants and bars in which to enjoy anything from the Peninsula's signature Cantonese delicacies to a light meal on one of the largest terraces in Paris. The rooftop restaurant L'Oiseau Blanc also offers romantic dining with 360-degree views of the capital.

Despite the 100-year-old façade of this former Ministry of Foreign Affairs building, the spacious rooms are as contemporary as they come thanks to a recent revamp by Hong Kong designer Henry Leung. Each room has a tablet computer that can be used to control the amenities in the room, contact the concierge service, and learn more about what to do while in town.

Luxury-conscious travellers can opt for The Peninsula Suite, which at 318 sq m is the largest in Paris. Guests of this room are taken for a spin around the city in a chauffeur-driven Mini Cooper.
19 Avenue Kléber, 75116
+33 (0)1 5812 2888
paris.peninsula.com

MONOCLE COMMENT: American composer George Gershwin was inspired by the sights and sounds of 1920s Paris and wrote his famous melody "An American in Paris" while staying here.

Glass act

The lobby art is called 'Dancing Leaves'

Food and drink

Bon appétit

The traditional Parisian food scene is not one that typically leans towards accommodating the desires of its diners: many restaurants have set times to eat and set menus to eat from. Luckily, the sheer quality, ambition and beauty of the food compensates for any rigidity you might encounter. And how could you not eat well in a country that has such a rich boutique produce industry and that's home to more than 400 distinct types of cheese?

Lingering over a meal is a national pastime and even lunch can span several hours. Conversations unfurl over protracted periods, mixing with wine and ending with coffee (which is thankfully becoming far better in quality).

Whether it's a bistro out of the last century or a sophisticated fine-dining venue, the larger-than-life reputation of French cuisine expresses itself in innumerable ways. We guarantee our selection here won't leave you hungry or blasé.

Restaurants
La dégustation

1

Café de la Nouvelle Mairie, Latin Quarter (5e)
Quintessential bistro

This neighbourhood favourite near Le Panthéon was taken over in 2000 by former waiter Benjamin Fourty and his partner Corentin Bucillat. It can be difficult to find a seat in the two small rooms: during the day the charmingly worn wooden tables fill with professors and students from the nearby Sorbonne, while at night people come from all over to enjoy the traditional French menu and sip wine at the zinc-topped bar.

The chalkboard changes daily but there are always seven starters – such as oysters from Normandy in winter and seasonal soup – quiche for lunch and meaty mains such as *côte de boeuf*. "We use only fresh produce and organic vegetables and we know all our suppliers," says Fourty. "Everything comes from France exclusively." The wine list is also a point of pride. "We only serve natural wines, 30-year-old bottles," he says. "We were one of the first restaurants in Paris to do so."
19 Rue des Fossés Saint-Jacques, 75005
+33 (0)1 4407 0441

New tricks
The bistro was formerly a canteen for clowns

2

Le Clown Bar, Oberkampf (11e)
Playfully inventive cuisine

This quirky bistro is decorated and named in honour of the clowns who would come here to eat and drink after performing in the rings at the nearby Cirque d'Hiver. Sven Chartier and Ewen Lemoigne, of the well-known Saturne restaurant, opened Le Clown Bar in 2014 after a makeover and installed former Vivant chef Atsumi Sota in the kitchen. Today the belle époque-era interior, with its painted circus figures somersaulting across the mirrored walls, is a fitting backdrop for the culinary whirls and turns Sota takes with his creative, modern French à la carte menu.
114 Rue Amelot, 75011
+33 (0)1 4355 8735
clown-bar-paris.com

Bones are so passé; vive la Paris-Brest pastry

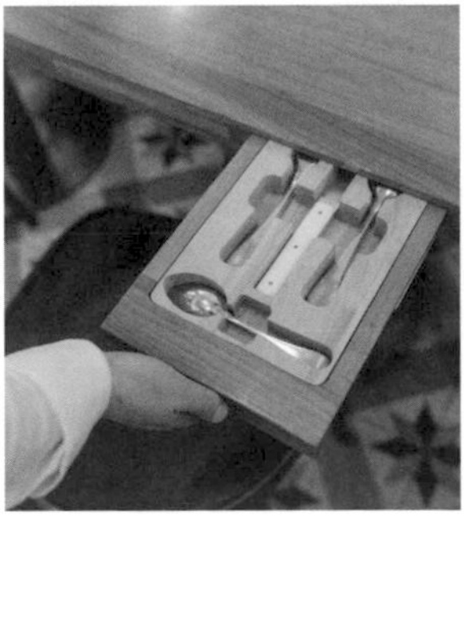

③

Ober Mamma, Oberkampf (11ᵉ)
Italian cooking lesson

This restaurant and cocktail bar is the second to launch under the Big Mamma group umbrella. It's the place to head if you fancy a break from rich French fare in favour of an authentic wood-fired pizza or pasta. "Here most Italian restaurants are trying to please French tongues," says co-founder Tigrane Seydoux. "They will add cream to the carbonara because French people like cream. We will teach the French how to eat Italian." If you're in the mood for something a little lighter, take a seat at the zinc-topped cocktail bar and order some small plates.
107 Boulevard Richard Lenoir, 75011
+33 (0)1 5830 6278
bigmammagroup.com

④

La Cave à Michel, Belleville (10ᵉ)
Lively tapas hotspot

Don't expect to find a seat at this busy bar near the Canal Saint-Martin. In the evening this petite wine shop transforms into a standing-room-only space headed by sommelier Fabrice Mansouri and chef Romain Tischenko, who dashes over from his neighbouring bistro Le Galopin to dish up the small plates while Mansouri pours from his 300-strong wine collection.

Listen to Mansouri's stories while savouring seasonal small plates heaped with grilled octopus, artichokes and Galician beef.
36 Rue Sainte-Marthe, 75010
+33 (0)1 4245 9447

Institutions

Sure, they may be old-fashioned, a little on the stuffy side and heavy on the wallet, but there's a reason why Paris has so many restaurants that have stood the test of time. Here is our pick of the icons of the culinary scene.

01 **Le Duc, Montparnasse:** Known as much for its boat-like aesthetic as its dishes made with fresh seafood from the coast of Brittany, Le Duc has been a staple since the 1960s. Its signature cooking style is *à la vapeur* ("steamed"): the turbot is a highlight.
restaurantleduc.com

02 **Caviar Kaspia, Madeleine:** A Parisian landmark that marries French chic with Russian tradition, Caviar Kaspia has been serving up caviar, blini and smoked seafood delicacies to celebrities and aristocrats since it was founded in 1927 by Russian émigré Arcady Fixon.
caviarkaspia.com

03 **Le Voltaire, Saint-Germain-des-Prés:** This restaurant overlooks the Seine from the Left Bank and is a favourite among the social set, especially during Paris Fashion Week. While the *côte de boeuf* is renowned, another speciality is the egg-mayonnaise dish "James", named after a wartime GI and favourite client.
+33 (0)1 4261 1749

04 **Josephine 'Chez Dumonet', Saint-Germain-des-Prés:** This archetypal bistro opened in 1880 and has been turning out authentic French cuisine (think homemade terrine, steak tartare and duck confit) since. Its art nouveau dining room gets very busy.
+33 (0)1 4548 5240

5

Le Verre Volé,
Canal Saint-Martin (10e)
Neighbourhood favourite

This former wine cellar morphed into a restaurant in 2000. With its red-tiled floors, tiny tables and battered chairs there's nothing slick about it but it has a warm atmosphere and is always packed with a lively crowd. "We're a little bit rock'n'roll," says owner Cyril Bordarier. "Our clients are people that know food and like to eat."

Made in-house, meals are based on organic vegetables, meat and seafood and change daily. Waiters on hand to help you explore the wine list are another bonus. There is also a wine cellar and *épicerie* in the 11e.
67 Rue de Lancry, 75010
+33 (0)1 4803 1734
leverrevole.fr

6

Le Chateaubriand,
Canal Saint-Martin (11e)
Bistronomie at its finest

The charm and aesthetic of this restaurant is that of an old-style neighbourhood bistro but its reputation is world-renowned. With French-Basque chef Inaki Aizpitarte (*pictured*) at the helm, Le Chateaubriand hasn't seen an empty table since its founding in 2006 (bookings must be made at least 21 days in advance). If you do get a table, don't fill up on the bread as the set menu is a hearty affair: a series of amuse-bouche followed by three mains, with cheese or dessert to finish.
129 Avenue Parmentier, 75011
+33 (0)1 4357 4595
lechateaubriand.net

Must-try
Soupe à l'oignon from Flottes, Tuileries
No trip is complete without a bowl of this iconic dish. We recommend Flottes, where the *gratinée* onion soup is topped with a gooey layer of gruyère cheese. Parisians will eat this after a late night out but it's delicious any time.
flottes.fr

7

Au Passage, Oberkampf (11^{e})
Informal expertise

The sharing plates at Au Passage give vegetables special attention (although offal is not shied away from either). Order swiftly: options dwindle as the night progresses. The tatty-chic interior underscores the restaurant's laidback approach to food and its clear mastery of it.
1 Bis Passage Saint-Sébastien, 75011
+33 (0)1 4355 0752
restaurant-aupassage.fr

8

David Toutain, Invalides (7e)
Cutting-edge cuisine

Toutain began his career at L'Arpège (*see page 34*) and went on to the hotplates at haute cuisine temples l'Ambroisie and l'Agapé Substance, before launching this venue in late 2013. The modish dining room is a fitting setting for the modern cuisine.

Diners can choose from a three-part set menu at lunch or a carte blanche tasting menu. Plate after plate introduces surprising flavour and texture combinations, perhaps best illustrated via a snapshot of some of his desserts: celery confit; cauliflower mousse with coconut; and pralined Jerusalem artichoke.
29 Rue Surcouf, 75007
+33 (0)1 4550 1110
davidtoutain.com

9

Clamato, Bercy (11^{e})
Seafood with spice

Clamato is a drink made of tomato-juice and clam broth, good for adding a briny twist to a Bloody Mary. Here, it's a popular *fisheria* headed up by the folks behind Michelin-starred Septime. Reservations aren't taken, so arrive no later than 19.00 to claim a spot in the minimalist dining room.

The tin crockery may look like it should be used around a campfire but it's not an accurate indicator of the sophistication of the food; regular menu items include deftly marinated fish and silky crab-fritters. The oysters, sourced from Normandy when in season, are another highlight.
80 Rue de Charonne, 75011
+33 (0)1 4372 7453
septime-charonne.fr

10

Le Baratin, Belleville (20ᵉ)
More than chat

Baratin means "smooth talker" in French but this cool and collected bistro is also backed up by substantial fare. A favourite of notable chefs such as Inaki Aizpitarte and Alain Ducasse, it's the exception in a neighbourhood that is otherwise characterised by Asian restaurants.

The menu of chef Raquel Carena (*pictured, on left*) is scribbled on a chalkboard. Her husband Philippe Pinoteau oversees the bistro's wine offering; he's gruff but he knows his way around the top-notch list, which has an accent on independent natural wines. Expect hearty options such as rabbit ragout and guinea hen.
3 Rue Jouye-Rouve, 75020
+33 (0)1 4349 3970

11

Ma Cocotte, Saint-Ouen
Hidden treasure

This restaurant is located in a converted warehouse at the heart of the city's best flea market, the Marché aux Puces de Saint-Ouen. The brainchild of ubiquitous French designer Philippe Starck, this 250-seat restaurant is split over two storeys. On the ground floor is the kitchen and a large dining room; upstairs there's a second eating area and cocktail bar decorated to make you feel as if you're stepping into someone's apartment. The eclectic furniture has all been sourced from the surrounding market and the result is a relaxed, homely vibe.

Its popularity has helped turn this unlikely local into one of the places to be seen in Paris. Yet despite this the food is hearty and unpretentious; roast chicken, fish and chips and burgers are perfect for filling up after an intensive antiquing session.
106 Rue des Rosiers, 93400
+33 (0)1 4951 7000
macocotte-lespuces.com

Quick lunch

01 **Café Ineko, Le Marais:** This spot, opened by Louis Vuitton graduate Inès de Villeneuve, has a decidedly Mediterranean vibe. The vegetarian-oriented menu is as light and pleasant as the eclectic decor, with regularly changing options. Alongside simple breakfast staples are filling lunch plates such as couscous with roasted beetroots, grilled fennel and king oyster mushrooms.
+33 (0)9 6787 2310

02 **Holiday Café, Porte de Saint-Cloud:** Beyond the immediate centre but worth the trip, this café (with an elegant interior by Atelier Franck Durand) is the brainchild of the eponymous *Holiday* magazine: a seminal mid-century US publication that was relaunched in 2014. The dishes – *croque demoiselle* or, for the sweet-toothed, apple compote – are warming, classic and well presented.
holiday-magazine.com/cafe

03 **Les Deux Abeilles, Champ de Mars:** The floral wallpaper, wooden furnishings and white tablecloths make this neighbourhood spot near the Eiffel Tower feel homely, like a great aunt's tea parlour. The courtyard is also an inviting space to linger over lunch on a sunny day. A variety of simple dishes such as quiches and lentil salads can be paired with classic desserts, including lemon tart, tiramisu and meringues. Wash it all down with some homemade lemonade.
+33 (0)1 4555 6404

(12)

Anahi, Le Marais (3e)

South American treasure

Monaco-born Riccardo Giraudi (*pictured*) is the meat-loving maestro behind the revival of this Parisian-Argentinian institution, where you're guaranteed a tasty Kobe beef taco or Wagyu empanadas. Architecture firm Humbert & Poyet has updated the decor and transformed the back of the dining room into a cocktail bar, which slings the best margaritas in town.

The result is a warm and intimate atmosphere that becomes even more cosy when it fills to the brim on weekends, and it stays that way until late.

49 Rue Volta, 75003
+33 (0)1 8381 3800
anahi-paris.com

13

Vivant, Poissonnière (10e)
Wine and dine

Vivant is a *cave à manger* – a wine shop that doubles as a bar, inviting thirsty patrons to drink top-notch tipple at non-restaurant prices. The sole catch is that you have to order something to nibble as you sip but, with young chef Pierre Touitou (*pictured right*) at the top of his game, it's hardly an onerous request.

While sommelier Felix Godart uncorks the bottles, Touitou serves a small menu that regularly features mouth-watering charcuterie, vegetable dishes such as celery with egg and pomelo, and heartier options that range from guinea fowl to suckling pig with polenta. Grab a seat at the marble-top bar and watch the young prodigy at work.
43 Rue des Petites Écuries, 75010
+33 (0)1 4246 4355
vivantparis.com

14

L'Arpège, Invalides (7e)
Vegetable worship

Chef Alain Passard cut his teeth in Michelin-starred restaurants in France and Belgium before opening L'Arpège in 1986. His own stars soon heaped up: number three was awarded in 1996. Passard's cuisine underwent a radical shift with the advent of his first kitchen garden, and now his daily vegetarian set menu is based on what is fresh. Quality ingredients, imagination and superb cooking skills all combine in dishes marked by their innovative flavour combinations; the humble beetroot, raspberry and carrot are elevated to new heights.
84 Rue de Varenne, 75007
+33 (0)1 4705 0906
alain-passard.com

15

Galliká Hellenic Foodies, Madeleine (9e)
Kebabs with flair

This upmarket Greek kebab shop fills up quickly (even if you arrive before opening time at 11.45 you'll probably have to queue) but the snappy service means that the line moves quickly. The bright-blue exterior leads into a simple dining space adorned with geometric tiles, flowerpots and wooden furnishings.

Galliká serves wraps brimming with tzatziki, halloumi, roast lamb and Greek salad; it's street food of the highest order. Just keep in mind that it's only open on weekends – and for just over three hours.
7 Rue Godot de Mauroy, 75009
+33 (0)9 5388 8375
gallika.fr

16

La Bourse et la Vie, Bourse (2e)
Second blooming

Daniel Rose, the American-born chef behind the venerable restaurant Spring one arrondissement over, has opened this upmarket bistro that puts the spotlight on gourmet ingredients. His French wife, chef Marie-Aude Mery, runs the tiny kitchen, which is open for breakfast, lunch and dinner (a rarity in Paris).

Dishes are classic and masterful: leeks with vinaigrette, peppery steak frites, pot-au-feu and crème caramel. The polished-metal-and-mirrors interior is certainly chicer than the prototypical bistro too.
12 Rue Vivienne, 75002
+33 (0)1 4260 0883
labourselavie.com

Must-try
Pavé du Mail from Chez Georges, Bourse
With its old wooden façade, dimly lit interior and lines of tables packed end to end, this classic French bistro is a little shabby around the edges but that's part of the charm. From the simple meat-heavy menu our pick is this house speciality: a juicy filet mignon steak doused in a creamy mustard and cognac sauce served with a heap of golden, crispy frites. There's a reason why *The New York Times* tapped this as one of the best places in Paris to get a steak.
+33 (0)1 4260 0711

Pâtisseries
Sweet treats

1

Bontemps Pâtisserie, Le Marais (3e)
Shortbread salvation

Every day the vitrine of Bontemps is adorned with fresh flowers and beautiful pâtisseries laid out on vintage cake stands. The *sablé* (shortbread) is incomparable, with flavourful fillings such as organic Sicilian lemon and homemade praline. The tartlets are almost too pretty to eat, made from organic figs from the south of France or simply perfect pure rounds of chocolate. Owner Fiona Leluc has been credited with bringing the once-unfashionable shortbread biscuit back into vogue; sample some of her sweet products to find out why.
57 Rue de Bretagne, 75003
+33 (0)1 4274 1068

Chilled out

Berthillon is celebrated for its ice cream and sorbets that combine both traditional and surprising flavours (such as caramel and pear, Armagnac and prune). The parfait for the maker's 60th anniversary was such a hit, it's now a bestseller: vanilla, passion fruit and Nepalese timut pepper.
berthillon.fr

2

Pâtisserie du Panthéon,
Latin Quarter (5e)
High-end treats

Sébastien Dégardin spent years working as a *pâtissier* in kitchens in Moscow, Dubai, Japan and Hong Kong before settling down in Paris. His home since 2013 has been a heritage-listed building, where he's created a warm interior that's a pleasant mix of classic and modern.

Choose a homemade brioche bun or the traditional Paris-Brest. Better yet, grab a selection and head to the nearby Jardin du Luxembourg.
200 Rue Saint-Jacques, 75005
+33 (0)1 4307 7759
sebastien-degardin.com

Tea and cakes

01 Mariage Frères, Saint-Germain-des-Prés: An authority on tea since 1854, its offerings span from the Ruschka (a Russian afternoon tea) to Thé au Sahara (green tea with mint and rose petals). All the accoutrements for tea making and drinking are available too: tea pots and strainers, plus the brand's classic lacquered tins.
mariagefreres.com

02 Mamie Gâteaux, Saint-Germain-des-Prés: If you're in need of comfort, this is the spot. A cast-iron stove and checked tablecloths create a cosy vibe for desserts and pastries made by Mariko Duplessis.
mamie-gateaux.com

Bakeries
Brilliant brunches

1

Du Pain et des Idées,
Canal Saint-Martin (10e)
Historic loaves

Baker Christophe Vasseur took over this neighbourhood establishment in 2002, saving the century-old bakery from disappearing. He and his team are committed to preserving its traditions: they work only by hand and bake on natural stone. The loaves of organic sourdough are baked from wheat, spelt, rye and chestnut and the seasonal fruit tarts rotate between Mouna apples, figs and peaches. Once you've made your purchases, go around the corner to the right and peer through the pale blue door to glimpse the masters at work.
34 Rue Yves Toudic, 75010
+33 (0)1 4240 4452
dupainetdesidees.com

Other bakeries

01 Blé Sucré, Bastille: Fabrice Le Bourdat makes some of the best croissants, desserts and breads in town. Formerly the pastry chef at the three-Michelin-starred restaurant Le Bristol, he now specialises in *mille-feuilles* (vanilla slices), iced madeleines, *financiers* (small sponge fingers) and Breton cakes.
+33 (0)1 4340 7773

02 Chambelland, Oberkampf: This gluten-free pâtisserie leaves allcomers satisfied, no matter their dietary preferences. The rice and buckwheat breads are made using flour from its own mill. Sandwiches are on the menu, along with lemon meringue, walnut tarts and the Browkie (a brownie-cookie hybrid).
chambelland.com

Only the brest

The Paris-Brest is a circular piece of crisp choux pastry cut in two and filled with rich hazelnut cream. Inspired by the Paris-Brest bicycle race that passed by his pâtisserie, chef Louis Durand invented the wheel-shaped treat in 1910.

2

Liberté, Canal Saint-Martin (10e)

Bakery with style

Benoît Castel, formerly at La Grande Épicerie du Bon Marché, has created a very design-minded patisserie-boulangerie: think polished marble and floor-to-ceiling vitrines. If you're looking for a quick lunch it's a good option; the menu includes sandwiches and salads, in addition to all the usual suspects such as croissants, breads, cakes and biscuits. The bakery acknowledges its fashionable clientele from the adjacent Saint-Canal area with an aptly named specialty treat: the *bobo au rhum* is a dessert that comes with a pipette of rum.

39 Rue de Vinaigriers 75010
+33 (0)1 4205 5176
libertepatisserieboulangerie.com

Small plates and wine
Standing-room only

1

L'Avant Comptoir, Saint-Germain-des-Prés (6e)

Bustling tapas bar

"We wanted it to be about people," says L'avant Comptoir's bar manager Eric Guibert about chef Yves Camdeborde's tapas-style wine bar. "It's something that has disappeared; it used to be so common in France during the 20th century."

The bar, tucked away behind an inconspicuous crêpe stand, was indeed designed to foster conversation: there are no menu cards to hide behind and the space is so tight that it evokes the sense of being a piece in a giant jigsaw puzzle as people step in and out of the narrow space. Aside from all the people when it's busy, the room is dominated by the zinc bar, towering wine displays and the night's dishes listed on flyers dangling from the ceiling. It's chaotic but wonderful.

3 Carrefour de l'Odéon, 75006
+33 (0)1 4427 0750

Brunch
Pick of the top tables

2

Aux Deux Amis, Oberkampf (11e)
Small things

David Vincent-Loyola's wine bar and bistro on Rue Oberkampf has made a name for itself thanks to its flavoursome home-cooked dishes and expertly picked natural wines. By-the-glass options are listed on old mirrors hung on tiled walls. On balmy Friday nights the crowd moves out onto the street. If you're lucky you'll score a coveted table and be able to tuck in to an order of the restaurant's signature *tortilla de janine* (ham with grilled almonds), *cheval tartare* (horse tartare) or fresh shucked oysters.
45 Rue Oberkampf, 75011
+33 (0)1 5830 3813

MAISON PLISSON
All in one
You can also pick up bread, meat and cheese

1

Maison Plisson, Le Marais (3e)
Baked goods and more

This bustling haunt near Le Marais' labyrinthine art and retail district fills mid-morning with chic gallery directors and clothing designers. The tarts and breads are delicious but if you're after something more substantial there are two daily dishes and a range of salads and sandwiches.

A bonus is that you can watch the bakers as they make the day's bread and pastries. The well-designed interiors, strong coffee and friendly staff mean your morning pit-stop can easily turn into an extended lunch.
93 Boulevard Beaumarchais, 75003
+33 (0)1 7118 1909
lamaisonplisson.com

I'm in danger of becoming a flightless bird

2

Claus, Louvre (1e)
Boutique brunch

If you're in the mood for something a little different to the typical Parisian breakfast of coffee and croissant eaten standing at a café bar, cut and run to Claus. On the ground floor of this minimalist two-storey café you'll find Bavarian-born owner Claus Estermann (*pictured on left*), presiding over a small number of tables and a delicatessen with a selection of homemade jams and *pains au chocolat*.

Upstairs there's more seating but book ahead: this is one of the most popular brunch spots in Paris. Diners can choose from a number of three-course breakfast menus packed with yoghurt and fruit compote, pastries, ham, smoked salmon, eggs and Saint-Nectaire cheese, even slices of gâteau (that's another thing we like about this place: cake is considered a breakfast food).

Be sure to also pop across the street to the recently opened Claus épicerie. It stocks cold-pressed juices, freshly ground coffee and other assorted gourmet breakfast goods for those who'd rather prepare their own at home.
14 Rue Jean-Jacques Rousseau, 75001
+33 (0)1 4233 5510
clausparis.com

Sumptuous stroll

From Tuesday to Sunday, Rue Mouffetard in the 5th arrondissement is lined with market stalls selling produce. Try Mococha at the bottom of the hill for bonbons by patissier Patrice Chapon, or sample local Brie de Meaux at 106-year-old fromagerie Androuet.
Latin Quarter

Japanese restaurants
Favourite spots

1

Kunitoraya, Louvre (1^{e})
Ca-noodling around

The udon noodle, humble yet tasty fare, is a staple in southeastern Japan. This noodle spot is worth its high price tag thanks to chef Masafumi Nomoto, who prepares the udon dough by hand. The lunch menu remains unchanged throughout the year and at night a seasonal fixed-price menu covers three entrées, a fried dish, udon, a chargrilled dish and a dessert.

One highlight includes poached oysters with caviar; white truffles are integrated in summer menus. The decor is a somewhat startling contrast: a bistro aesthetic with white tiling and vintage mirrors, the remnants of when the venue was known as Chez Paulette.
5 Rue Villedo, 75001
+33 (0)1 4703 0774
kunitoraya.com

Heritage wander

You'll find some of the legends of French cuisine along Rue Montorgueil, a pedestrian-only street near Sentier Station. Try snails at L'Escargot Montorgueil (open since 1832); baked goods at the city's oldest pâtisserie Stohrer; and oysters at 200-year-old Au Rocher de Cancale.

I love my morning strolls down Rue Montorgueil

2

Nanashi, Le Marais (3^{e})
Quick and easy bentos

Chef Kaori Endo (*pictured*) wanted to offer fresh Japanese food with a French twist in a casual setting – and this is exactly what is on offer at Nanashi in buzzing Le Marais. The signature dishes are the lunchtime bento boxes, which come in meat, fish and vegetarian options on a bed of wild rice or quinoa with a serving of salad and vegetables.

The daily menu makes the most of seasonal provisions but a typical box might contain tofu galette, wasabi-white-cheese or ricotta-stuffed zucchini. Even the puddings – black sesame panna cotta, matcha cake – sound as though they might be healthy. In the evening, the shift is to a more Japanese tapas style with the chirashi salmon and soba-noodle dishes particularly recommended. The clean, white decor and primary colours hint at Scandinavia, making this a truly cosmopolitan experience.
57 Rue Charlot, 75003
+33 (0)9 6000 2559
nanashi.fr

Two more

01 **Soma, Le Marais:** This small restaurant serves Japanese cuisine tempered with Gallic cooking methods and ingredients: clams in saké and French toast with green-tea ice cream. Chef Sourasack Phongphet of award-winning Ploum works in an open kitchen in the middle of the room, creating an inclusive vibe. If you're up for it, try the live-fried Madagascan prawns that still wriggle on the plate.
lesoma.fr

02 **Udon Jubey, Pyramides:** Don't be fooled by the functional exterior: this small but popular canteen-style restaurant offers the tastiest Japanese food at agreeable prices in the Little Tokyo district. Its udon noodles are served hot or cold in a choice of broths: beef curry, prawn tempura, pork or soya. Grab a seat at the counter to watch the efficient chefs work their magic in the open kitchen.
+33 (0)1 4015 9254

Gourmet produce
Choice craftsmanship

1

Fromagerie Barthélemy, Saint-Germain-des-Prés (7e)
Cheese-lover heaven

No fridges, branding or use-by dates can be found in Fromagerie Barthélemy, only wall-to-wall cheese. Owner Nicole Barthélemy has been in the business for more than 40 years and believes it's better to have a small shop overflowing than a big store near bare. Famed for her Fontainebleau, the Madame of cheese has supplied *fromage* to the Élysée Palace and the prime minister's residence since the 1970s.

More than 200 varieties, mostly made from raw milk, are stored and released only when ready. Rumour has it Barthélemy sells one tonne of Mont d'Or every few months, requiring a full-time staffer dedicated solely to caring for this soft cheese.
51 Rue de Grenelle, 75007
+33 (0)1 4222 8224

2

Les Épiciers, Rambuteau (3e)
Brothers in hams

Friends Selim Ben Attia and Pierre Chambouleyron (*pictured, Attia on left*) have created more than just a gourmet grocer. Regional produce from Baulois fondants to Pierre Moncuit champagne, as well as the mandatory cornucopia of hams and cheeses, is stocked throughout the day. Come afternoon there's a delectable menu of sandwiches and salads – don't miss the goat's cheese, honey and Périgord nuts on toasted baguette – and in the evening the shop turns into a wine bar, serving bottles by the glass and towering charcuterie platters.
33 Rue de Montmorency, 75003
+33 (0)9 5050 2067
les-epiciers.com

Two more

01 Chocolatier Arnaud Larher, Saint-Germain-des-Prés: A master of his art, Arnaud Larher is a patissier-chocolatier of the highest order. These chocolates, pastries and macaroons are as much works of art as they are food, but it is Larher's passion for taste experimentation that defines this haute pâtisserie. Search out one of three boutiques for sweet perfection.
arnaudlarher.com

02 Maison Verot, Saint-Germain-des-Prés: Hailing from a family of charcutiers, Gilles Verot has pork pedigree. Head to one of his and wife Catherine's three artisanal butcher shops for the finest pâtés, terrines, saucissons, *jambons* and other picnic delicacies. The pâté de Houdan (pâté in pastry with a pork and pistachio base) in particular is a porcine treat.
maisonverot.fr

Markets
Produce snapshot

1

Marché d'Aligre, Bastille (12e)
Biggest and best

This is a true neighbourhood market. Situated between Faubourg Saint-Antoine and Rue de Charenton, Marché d'Aligre has been catering for the working-class population of the area since the 18th century. It's still one of the most reasonably priced markets in Paris, though prices increase slightly on Saturdays and Sundays (as does the foot traffic).

The sellers vary widely from organic farmers and specialised herb stalls to bulk-style vendors; visit at the tail end and they're practically giving away their provisions. The market is also open six days a week; a liberal timeframe relative to other markets' twice-weekly custom. The outdoor stalls remain open until early afternoon; come 15.00, you'd never imagine such bounty had been here. The *marché* also contains a covered hall stocked with cheese shops, fishmongers, butchers, dry goods and beer- and wine-sellers.
Place d'Aligre, 75012
marchedaligre.free.fr

②
Marché Bio du Boulevard Raspail, Saint-Germain-des-Prés (6e)
Plethora of produce

This *marché* incorporates some 50 merchants and producers selling certified-organic products. The fruit- and vegetable-sellers are the most represented but there are also butchers, florists, wine-sellers and fishmongers.

Highlights include the honey at the Les Ruchers de Sologne stand and the gorgeous antipasti (olives, caperberries, artichokes) at the opposite stall. Small packets of *fleur de sel* (salt) flavoured with fennel or chilli make good gifts too. Don't miss the man at the end selling delicious galettes with potatoes, cheese and onions.
Boulevard Raspail, 75006

Market eats

Marché des Enfants Rouges dates back to 1615 and is Paris's oldest covered market. The strip of stalls, most with their own seating, are the spot for a taste of authentic French food. Try L'Estaminet for oysters and Versant Vins for a drink; it stocks more than 200 wines from France alone.

③
Marché du Président Wilson, Trocadéro (16e)
Cultural crop

Sandwiched between iconic Paris cultural institutions such as the Musée d'Art Moderne, Palais de Tokyo and Palais Galliera, this market's central location means that it's a popular haunt for tourists. But Parisians shop for their groceries here too.

Check out the selection of miniature vegetables (carrots, leeks) at vendor FLK; you'll see plenty of other heirloom varieties of fruit and veg across the markets. There are also flowers, baked goods and cheeses. If hunger strikes, hit up the excellent crêpe and Lebanese food stands.
Avenue du Président Wilson, 75116

Drinks
Sip in style

①
Paname Brewing Company, La Villette (19e)
Waterfront beers

This craft-beer brewery opened in 2015 in the up-and-coming 19th arrondissement. Its terrace overlooking the Bassin de la Villette is a good option for a brew on a sunny day. There are five house beers to work your way through – from the IPA Barge du Canal to the Pale Ale L'oeil de Biche and the Black Ale Bête Noire – that are poured straight from a tap connected to the beer barrels on show. Every month there's an exotic beer to sample that surprises; wildflower apricot and pumpkin have been past flavours.

The brewery is housed in an old grain-and-wine warehouse that dates from 1845. Michael Kennedy and his fellow co-founders are aspiring to bring back a little of the artisanship that existed in the craft-beer scene back then; so far, so good.
41 Bis Quai de la Loire, 75019
+33 (0)1 4036 4355
panamebrewingcompany.com

I'm getting into the swing of this 'natural wines' trend

Must-try
Champagne and oysters from Huîtrerie Régis, Saint-Germain-des-Prés
In a city that loves its bivalves it takes something special to stand out, but the ones at Huîtrerie Régis are true superstars. Sourced from the Marennes-Oléron region on France's west coast, they vary in size and rarity but all are served on a bed of ice with a twist of lemon. Little else is required apart from a glass (or bottle) from the excellent champagne and wine list (sancerres and muscadets are a speciality).
+33 (0)1 4441 1007

②

La Buvette, Parmentier (11e)

Little beauty

Follow the modest but alluring neon sign in the window to discover the wine list and minimalist decor put together by Camille Fourmont (*pictured*), who formerly managed the bar at Inaki Aizpitarte's Le Dauphin. Licensing laws mean eating with your drink is a requisite but that's no drawback here, where you can sample quality small plates from the menu scribbled on a mirror. The dishes are mostly cold snacks such as *sardinillas*, olives, cheese, terrine and finely sliced saucisson. Affordable bottles by independent producers are also for sale to take away.

67 Rue Saint Maur, 75011
+33 (0)9 8356 9411

③

Le Mary Celeste, Le Marais (3e)

Oysters and cocktails

This is another laudable establishment from the team behind hotspots Candelaria and Glass. "We don't force people to eat a meal – they can have a cocktail or a glass of wine and oysters," says its co-founder Carina Soto Velasquez.

The staff commandeer the space with authority, shaking drinks and shucking with gusto for those seated around the circular bar. The small room fills with diners by 20.00 so if you want a table or a bar seat, be sure to arrive early. We recommend the Troubadour cocktail, which blends Scotch with citrus flavours.

1 Rue Commines, 75003
lemaryceleste.com

④

Frenchie Bar à Vins, Bonne Nouvelle (2e)

Hole-in-the-wall bar

Chef Grégory Marchand's wine bar, on a small side street minutes from Sentier Metro station, opened just two years after the 2009 launch of his neighbouring restaurant Frenchie. Both establishments (as well as the takeaway lunch spot Frenchie to Go) were named after the moniker given to Marchand by British chef Jamie Oliver.

Reservations for the restaurant – which offers a five-course wine-pairing menu – are hard to come by but this more relaxed wine bar is open on a first-come, first-served basis. The room's brick walls, half-timbered ceiling and bottle-lined shelves make for a cosy spot to meet friends over a carafe of bordeaux. To accompany your tipple there's cheese from London's Neal's Yard Dairy and a very decent lobster roll.

5-6 Rue du Nil, 75002
+33 (0)1 4039 9619
frenchie-restaurant.com

Shore thing
Enjoy oysters fresh from Normandy on Sundays

5

Le Baron Rouge, Bastille (12e)

Working-class act

It can feel as if the entire neighbourhood is crammed into this blue-collar bar on weekend afternoons and weekday evenings. Le Baron Rouge is a boisterous and pretention-free spot for a post-market glass of wine, a plate of cheese or charcuterie or, in winter, a dozen oysters. Be prepared to elbow for room at the bar or crowd around a barrel or a stack of crates (here they double as tables). If you can't nudge in, head outside with the other latecomers using nearby window ledges and the bonnets of parked cars for alfresco consumption.

1 Rue Théophile Roussel, 75012

+33 (0)1 4343 1432

Wine bars

01 **Le Garde Robe, Louvre:** Bottles of natural, organic and biodynamic wines are available to take away from this bar and lined up for the picking in wooden cases. Those consumed on the premises attract a corkage fee. On warm days, grab a stool and charcuterie and cheese board and enjoy the sun.
+33 (0)1 4926 9060

02 **Le Rubis, Pyramides:** The wine list alone – spanning producers from Jo Landron to Julien Meyer – makes dropping in worth it but an equally weighted incentive is the menu of refined bistro classics such as *escalope de veau* and tuna tartare. Dishes are based on what's in season so they tend to change daily; provenance of the meats, cheeses, fish and vegetables is always cited. Ingredients are usually bought from the exceptional gastronomic enclave Terroirs d'Avenir nearby.
+33 (0)1 4261 0334

03 **Le Siffleur de Ballons, Bastille:** This bright and cheery two-room space is discreetly located near the Marché d'Aligre. The bottles on display are available to take away but for a corkage fee you can also make yourself comfortable at one of the tables. Diners can choose from plates of ultra-thin artisanal Spanish and Italian hams or tuck into a variety of small dishes, such as beluga lentils with truffle oil. The food menu is complemented by a well-selected list of wines by the glass, including côtes du rhône elodie balme and VDF brumes de lestignac.
lesiffleurdeballons.net

Late nights
Venues with a buzz

1

Le Montana,
Saint-Germain-des-Prés-(6e)
Hottest ticket in town

Like many of the fashionable night spots littered around Paris, historic Le Montana was recently given the kiss of life by a prominent team of local creatives: artist André Saraiva and *Purple* magazine editor Olivier Zahm. The plush interior fit out was handled by designer Vincent Darré.

What with all the fashionistas, models and celebrities jostling to get in, gaining access can be tricky – it helps to know the name of the hostess or have a room booked in the hotel upstairs. But once inside, you'll find a Studio 54-inspired micro-club that's likely to be hosting the best party to be found in the city that night. If you want to fit in with the chic crowd, order a piscine, Le Montana's signature drink of champagne on ice.
28 Rue Saint-Benoît, 75006
+33 (0)1 5363 7920
hotel-lemontana.com

Take the waters

During the 1980s, Les Bains Douche was a riotous nightclub where celebrities such as David Bowie, Mick Jagger and Boy George came to splash about in its bathing pools. It's been saved from extinction and overhauled; today it's a decadent hotel, restaurant and bar.
lesbains-paris.com

Nightclubs

01 **Chez Castel, Saint-Germain-des-Prés:** The red-walled restaurant-cum-club has been part of the Rive Gauche nightlife since the 1960s, when it was the hangout for the likes of Serge Gainsbourg and Jean-Paul Belmondo. The patrons today are no less renowned: Louis Vuitton held its afterparty there following a 2015 fashion week show.
castelparis.com

02 **Panic Room, Oberkampf:** This nightclub on the periphery of artsy Le Marais is the go-to for those who want to dance the night away without the pomp and ceremony of the Champs-Élysées. There's an inventive cocktail bar on the top floor while the downstairs holds the fluorescent club area, which hosts Parisian and international DJs.
panicroomparis.com

03 **Silencio, Bourse:** David Lynch's club houses a gallery, cinema, library, smoking room, two bars and a stage. It's members only until midnight but after that it bustles with a diverse crowd of Parisian creatives and intrigued foreigners. The interiors were designed by Lynch and the influence of his eerie sensibility is evident throughout.
silencio-club.com

Cafés
Bean counters

1
Ten Belles, Canal Saint-Martin (10e)
Brewing up a storm

Paris is no longer a city of second-rate coffee if this establishment is anything to go by. Ten Belles, run by chefs Anna Trattles and Alice Quillet, is something of a cult spot for bean-heads and on any given day punters gather at the front window, chatting among the blooms overflowing from the Bleuet Coquelicot florist next door. "Parisians have finally embraced third-wave coffee culture," says Quillet. Aside from full-bodied cappuccinos, soups, toasted sandwiches and baked goods are made daily in-house.
10 Rue de la Grange Aux Belles, 75010
+33 (0)1 4240 9078
tenbelles.com

French roast — Ten Belles has brought decent coffee to Paris

I'm an early bird so good coffee is essential

Coffee

The French tend to think of coffee as a drink to simply cap off a meal, which is perplexing given how conscientious they are when it comes to every other aspect of eating and drinking. In Paris, *le café* too often comes from automated vending machines or in the form of acrid offerings from corner bistros. But a new take on sourcing and brewing has resulted in some delicious results. It took a wave of foreigners from the UK, the US and Australia (as well as a few well-travelled French roasters) to create the coffee-as-craft attitude and get speciality coffee shops flourishing.

01 **Telescope, Pyramides:** Focusing expertly on coffee plus a handful of accompanying sweets, this is a caffeine-aficionado hub with a certain aura of solemnity. The spare decor is centred around a solid hardwood bar.
telescopecafe.com

02 **Honor, Madeleine:** Located in a charming courtyard, this café run by an Australian-born couple is housed in a modular kiosk fit for all weathers and seasons. Its coffee is supplemented by savoury tarts, sandwiches and cakes.
honor-cafe.com

03 **Fragments, Le Marais:** The wooden counter at the front of the shop is the spot to pick up single and double-shot cappuccinos. To the rear the rawness of the café's interior space, with unembellished brick walls and exposed wooden beams, is balanced by a range of homemade cakes along with a small menu of sweet and savoury toasts.
76 Rue de Tournelles, 75003

Retail
— A certain 'je ne sais quoi'

Paris is the world's leading fashion capital: it's the home of haute couture and its renowned luxury brands draw throngs of tourists to Avenue Montaigne and Avenue des Champs-Élysées. But the city is much more than an expensive gift shop: young and independent brands and concept stores are constantly popping up to stand next to the big names.

Paris has stayed true to its artisanal roots and practices; many of its makers, crafting everything from ceramics and glassware to leather goods, have been in business for centuries. Then there are the design galleries and the tumultuous flea markets to explore.

It can all be a tad overwhelming, so here we've compiled our pick of the retail options – so you won't have to think twice before embarking on your shopping spree.

Mixed fashion and concept
Perfect fits

① Merci, Le Marais (3e)
Thematic exploration

In 2009 Bernard and Marie-France Cohen, the husband-and-wife team who founded Bonpoint, opened Merci, a space that gathers quality clothing, design furniture and home essentials. The ground floor is also regularly given over to exhibitions that are built around themes that could be anything from the work of a particular designer to the output of a whole country.

"It's like a magazine: the exhibitions translate an editorial dimension to the brand," says Merci's Laurence Leclerc. "Recent themes have included 'slow life' – on diverse objects that make life easier – Danish design, fashion and food." The former wallpaper factory also houses a restaurant that faces a pretty garden on the lower level. "At Merci there is always something to see, to discover, to taste," adds Leclerc.
111 Boulevard Beaumarchais, 75003
+33 (0)1 4277 0033
merci-merci.com

② Lemaire, Le Marais (3e)
Discreet luxury

After years working as an assistant to Thierry Mugler, Yves Saint Laurent and Christian Lacroix, Christophe Lemaire launched his own brand in 1990. The practical and well-crafted clothes that he creates with partner Sarah-Linh Tran became an immediate hit.

Architect Franklin Azzi designed the shop to look like a Parisian apartment, with thick carpets and padded leather couches. It's the perfect setting for Lemaire's signature staples: elegant double-breasted jackets, straight-legged trousers and below-the-knee dresses.
28 Rue de Poitou, 75003
+33 (0)1 4478 0009
lemaire.fr

③

French Trotters, Le Marais (3e)
Modern staples

Founded in 2005 by husband and wife Clarent and Carole Dehlouz, French Trotters started as a multibrand shop featuring the couple's favourite ready-to-wear and lifestyle labels. Duly inspired, a couple of years later they decided to expand into men's and womenswear with their own line, specialising in simple, well-crafted and functional pieces.

Their new shop in the district of Le Marais mostly features the French Trotters line along with clothes and accessories by Our Legacy, Acne, Michel Vivien and Jérôme Dreyfuss. The homeware section offers products from Astier de Villatte and gorgeous linen from African brand Tensira. "We like to think of French Trotters as a global lifestyle brand," says Clarent. "It's a great way to combine all of our passions."
128 Rue Vieille du Temple, 75003
+33 (0)1 4461 0014
frenchtrotters.fr

④

The Broken Arm, Le Marais (3e)
Avant-garde wardrobe

In 2013, Anaïs Lafarge, Romain Joste and Guillaume Steinmetz opened this boutique in a quiet street in front of a small public garden. The Broken Arm stocks pieces for both men and women by established designers such as Raf Simons and Lemaire, along with up-and-coming labels including Jacquemus and Raphaëlla Riboud.

The friendly shop has its own café with a cosy atmosphere (think Formica tables, decorative tiles and vintage school chairs); making it a lovely place to take a break from an intense shopping schedule.
12 Rue Perrée, 75003
+33 (0)1 4461 5360
the-broken-arm.com

Tailored titles
The Broken Arm sells design books too

(5)

La Garçonnière, Bonne Nouvelle (2e)
Man's best friend

What started as a pop-up shop by a group of young entrepreneurs has become a permanent fixture in a two-storey building in the 2nd arrondissement. The concept store features 140 menswear brands, among them wallets from Apto, ties and cufflinks by Monsieur London and leather goods from Newstalk – brands originally started by the founders themselves.

Staying true to their ethos of accessibility, most of the range is reasonably priced, making La Garçonnière a real go-to rather than a one-off. Beyond the clothing you'll find a slick café – the perfect place to linger after the spree – and a small *épicerie* stocking wine, spirits and plenty of goodies for the pantry. Downstairs there's a co-working space and barbershop if a quick snip is in order.

40 Rue des Petits Carreaux, 75002
+33 (0)9 7368 1447
la-garconniere.fr

(6)

Maison Kitsuné, Le Marais (11e)
Effortless style

Maison Kitsuné's fourth Parisian shop is its most impressive. Founders Gildas Loaëc and Masaya Kuroki wanted the feel of a villa; Nicolas Dorval-Bory Architectes and architecture agency Haau decided on a marble staircase by Dzek and British designer Max Lamb as its centrepiece, while the aesthetic was inspired by David Hockney.

Upstairs you'll find a refined range of men's and womenswear that includes trench coats, printed shirts and wool sweaters. Café Kitsuné provides a pit-stop.

18 Boulevard des Filles du Calvaire, 75011
+33 (0)1 5830 1237
kitsune.fr

(7)

L'Eclaireur, Les Halles (1e)
Fashion's best-kept secret

When Armand Hadida opened L'Eclaireur in 1980 it was just one small shop buried in the basement of an art gallery. Since then the brand has grown to encompass six distinct boutiques, each with its own vision and aesthetic. It carries off-the-radar fashion for men and women that comes courtesy of designers including Paul Harnden, Boris Bidjan Saberi and Lamberto Losani; you can also buy jewellery, accessories and Fornasetti candles.

Of the six locations we've picked out the tucked-away L'Eclaireur Hérold, which is located on a quiet street inside the former horse stables of an 18th-century *hôtel particulier* (townhouse). "This shop goes against every marketing code that applies to luxury boutiques: it's a place you can't see from the street," says Hadida.

10 Rue Hérold, 75001
+33 (0)1 4041 0989
leclaireur.com

It's not hard to sniff out a chic outfit in Paris

Rich pickings — Hermès flagship store is suitably grand

8

Hermès, Madeleine (8e)
No horsing around

This iconic French label was founded in 1837 and became internationally renowned for crafting equestrian equipment before expanding into luxury luggage. The flagship shop is designed to impress: its four floors are given over to displaying the brand's tableware, silk scarves, handbags and ready-to-wear fashion. Hermès is also remaining true to its roots: a roster of in-house saddlers conduct repairs in a small workspace open to viewing by the public.
24, Rue du Faubourg Saint-Honoré, 75008
+33 (0)1 4017 4717
hermes.com

Luxury brands

01 Louis Vuitton: This brand is as synonymous with Paris fashion as it is with high-quality luggage: it began as a trunk-making workshop off Place Vendôme. No trip is complete without a visit to its grand Champs-Élysées flagship.
louisvuitton.com

02 Comme des Garçons: Since Comme des Garçons led the "Japanese invasion" of Paris Fashion Week in 1981, in which elusive designer Rei Kawakubo's all-black showing rocked the fashion world, the brand has called Paris home.
comme-des-garcons.com

03 Céline: Design heavyweight Phoebe Philo took the creative helm in 2008 and since then Céline has focused on pared-down womenswear with a contemporary edge. The flagship store is on Avenue Montaigne.
celine.com

04 Chanel: Coco Chanel established this luxury brand in the early 20th century and its influence has endured thanks to Karl Lagerfeld. He has kept things fresh while paying homage to the brand's illustrious history. The Rue Cambon shop is the model for every other Chanel boutique in the world.
chanel.com

05 Dior: Christian Dior revived French fashion in the late 1940s; now, with Kris Van Assche in charge, the brand provides both sexes with elegant threads. The boutique on Rue Royale is the place to buy them.
dior.com

Menswear
Timely tailoring

Stepping out
Derbies and moccasins are the house specialities

①
JM Weston, Champs-Élysées (8e)
Best foot forward

Founded in 1891 in Limoges by Edouard Blanchard, this is now one of France's most emblematic shoemakers. The brand opened its first shop in 1922 on the Boulevard de Courcelles, before settling on the Champs-Élysées 10 years later.

Today JM Weston continues to sell the brand's classic shoes, including the famous "180" moccasins, which have been popular since the 1960s. Made-to-order shoes are also available and there are more than 200 types of leather to choose from.
50 Avenue des Champs-Élysées, 75008
+33 (0)1 4562 2647
jmweston.fr

②
Hollington, Latin Quarter (6e)
Elegant workwear

Irish designer Patric Hollington has a simple approach to clothing design: he aims to create pieces that are elegant enough for the office yet comfortable enough to be worn every day. His eponymous label specialises in collarless tweed jackets with multiple pockets.

Also worth a look are Hollington's "Nehru" shirts, which are cut in either Liberty print cloth or plain cotton. This quiet, spacious shop also sells tasteful ties, socks and bags that add polish to any outfit.
9 Rue Racine, 75006
+33 (0)1 4325 5479
hollington.eu

③
De Fursac, Richelieu (2e)
Fashion with focus

Applying French tailoring to high-quality fabrics sourced from Italian clothiers such as Lanificio F.lli Cerruti, this brand turns out season after season of well-cut sweaters, suits and outerwear. There are outlets scattered around Paris but the standout is the first shop on a busy corner in the 2nd arrondissement. Its modern design echoes the cutting-edge creative direction of the brand. Sharp and considered, the pared-down displays put all the focus on the clean lines and quality fabrics of the clothes.
112 Rue de Richelieu, 75002
+33 (0)1 4296 6612
defursac.fr

④
Charvet, Place Vendôme (1er)
Made-to-measure heaven

This fashion house was founded in 1838 and the likes of Winston Churchill and Ernest Hemingway have all worn Charvet designs; this place is still unequalled when it comes to providing made-to-measure shirts in Paris. The second floor is a charming salon where clients have their measurements taken and choose from more than 5,000 fabrics that are displayed like books in a library (there are a staggering 500 different tones of white to peruse). The shirts are then whipped up in the workrooms on the upper floors.
28 Place Vendôme, 75001
+33 (0)1 4260 3070
charvet.com

⑤
Ami, Le Marais (3^e)
Your new best friend

Launched in 2011 by designer Alexandre Mattiussi, this shop on the tree-lined Boulevard Beaumarchais is the brand's first outpost. The minimal space designed by Studio KO (the folks behind London restaurant Chiltern Firehouse) has the feel of a Parisian loft apartment and is warmed by leather-topped oak tables and brass fixtures.

Mattiussi once worked at Givenchy and Dior, and Ami reflects this experience: traditional styles and fabrics with a modern edge but at a lower price point.
109 Boulevard Beaumarchais, 75003
+33 (0)9 8327 6528
amiparis.fr

❻
Victoire Barber and Shop, Poissonnière (10e)
The whole story

When Franck Gauthé, Nissad Golampeer and Boubacar Gueye couldn't find any Parisian menswear shops they liked, they decided to create their own. "We wanted it to be a men's cultural centre that has everything one needs," says Gauthé.

The space, which they designed themselves (including the furniture), is divided in two. One side offers a consistently solid clothing section featuring pieces from Private White VC and Gitman, plus books and accessories. The other half is a barber shop, where you can get a clean shave or haircut. "People who make an appointment get to do a little shopping and vice-versa; it's a good combination," says Gauthé.
96 Rue du Faubourg Poissonnière, 75010
+33 (0)1 4016 4020
victoirebarberandshop.fr

Best foot forward

Berluti has been producing footwear for more than 100 years. In-store consultants measure your foot so that your new Venezia-leather bespoke shoes will fit perfectly – in turn ensuring that they will be worth the hefty price tag.
berluti.com

Department stores

01 **Le Bon Marché, Saint-Germain-des-Prés:** This was built in 1852 and was the city's first department store. Its founder, Aristide Boucicaut, pioneered modern services such as item exchange and home delivery. Today the space holds everything you could imagine wanting to buy, including a huge collection of shoes and the renowned Grande Épicerie, where customers can purchase gourmet food from all over the world.
lebonmarche.com

02 **Printemps, Haussmann:** Founded in 1865, this was the first shop to have lifts and establish the concept of marked-down prices on past collections. Now its art nouveau dome looms large over a range of luxury brands and beauty products. Fashion enthusiasts should not miss the Maria Luisa section, featuring pieces from emerging talents.
printemps.com

03 **Galeries Lafayette, Haussmann:** The world's busiest department store is on most tourists' bucket lists with good reason. Inside the incredible art nouveau building (*see page 118*), huge areas are given over to luxury accessories, beauty products and children's toys. Most French brands have outposts here and the shop's grocery section, Lafayette Gourmet, is a must-see for a snapshot of high-end produce. The centre also has a cultural space where it presents four exhibitions a year.
galerieslafayette.com

⑦
Officine Générale, Saint-Germain-des-Prés (6e)
Material wealth

Tailored workwear is the speciality of this brand founded in 2012 by Pierre Mahéo, who honed his skills working for prêt-a-porter studios such as Arthur & Fox. His Oxford shirts are now integral to many a stylish Parisian wardrobe. "I put the priority on the quality of the fabric," he says.

Mahéo sources his thin poplin from Italy, while his fresco fabric comes from Savile Clifford in England. His denim, jersey and Oxford materials are from Japan. "It's more expensive but it's the best in the world," he says.
6 Rue du Dragon, 75006
+33 (0)9 8253 3888
officinegenerale.com

Womenswear and accessories
Dress to impress

❶
Delvaux, Palais-Royal (1e)
Fit for a queen

Delvaux was founded in 1829 and has been an official supplier of bags to the Royal Court of Belgium since 1883. The brand set its first Parisian flagship under the Palais-Royal arcades at the end of 2014; inside, the modern furniture contrasts with details from the past, including a staircase borrowed from the Lumière brothers' film studio.

The shop displays numerous elegant handbags, from the lady-like "Brillant" to the iconic "Tempête". Men have their fair share of goods to choose from too: the briefcases are particularly noteworthy.
151-154 Galerie de Valois, 75001
+33 (0)9 6719 9328
delvaux.com

❷
Vanessa Seward, Louvre (1e)
Sound choice

Vanessa Seward worked with Karl Lagerfeld and Tom Ford before launching her own brand in 2015. Her boutique is an interesting space for her feminine, minimalist clothing; we also love the music, specially chosen by her husband, composer Bertrand Burgalat.
10 Rue d'Alger, 75001
+33 (0)1 8565 8889
vanessaseward.com

③
Goyard, Louvre (1e)
Travel in style

It's been almost 200 years since Goyard settled in a shop that has played host to the likes of Romy Schneider, Pablo Picasso and Édith Piaf. Browse the famous "Goyardine" printed trunks, suitcases and trolleys, along with purses, briefcases and wallets.
233 Rue Saint-Honoré, 75001
+33 (0)1 4260 5704
goyard.com

Clean lines

The flagship store has a utilitarian backdrop

④
Inès de la Fressange, Saint-Germain-des-Prés (7e)
C'est chic

After much legal wrangling, this Inès de la Fressange boutique opened in 2015. The shop's aesthetic is based on a hardware store and presents an effortlessly laidback selection of clothes, shoes, bags and scarves.

"We want this to be a more enjoyable form of luxury: more affordable and easier to wear," says Fabrice Boé, the man responsible for relaunching the brand and reinstalling the designer herself as creative director.

24 Rue de Grenelle, 75007
+33 (0)1 4548 1906
inesdelafressange.fr

To the letter

Jean Touitou's Parisian label APC has been putting out well-tailored clothing for men and women since 1987. What started as a small utilitarian brand soon grew into a fully fledged outfit, known for its premium raw denim. Head to any of eight Paris shops.
apc.fr

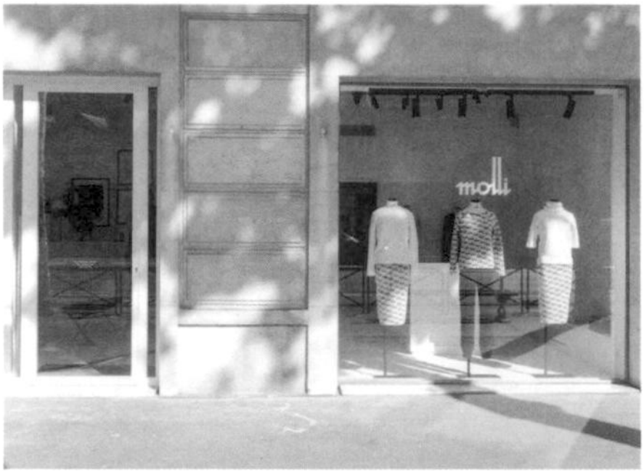

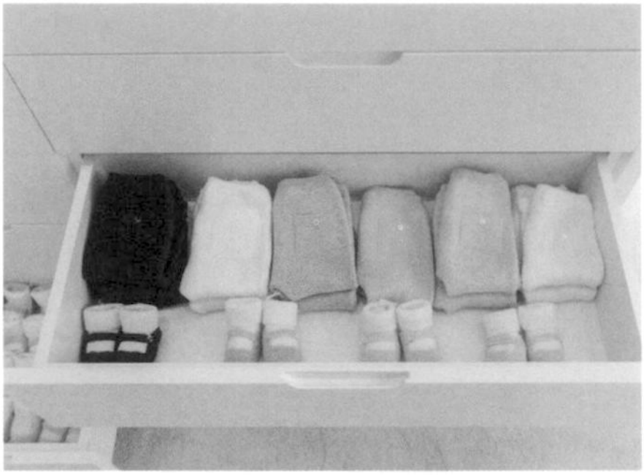

Branching out

Molli stocks both women's and children's clothes

Well, isn't this a nice place to have a rest...

5

Molli, Saint-Germain-des-Prés (7e)
Established pattern

It's unusual to pop into a shop for a gift and end up leaving with the keys to the company but that's essentially what happened to Charlotte de Fayet (*pictured*). Previously the marketing manager at L'Oréal and Danone, the mother of two decided to swap careers after buying a gift for her newborn at Molli, a much-loved childrenswear brand specialising in beautiful handmade knitwear.

The airy shop now sells a womenswear line that is modelled on the luxury feel and clean lines of the infant collection but with bolder designs in the powder-coloured mix. "My idea was to reawaken Molli's most beautiful items by emphasising the iconic moss stitch that is knitted with double-needle bars to produce its unique texture," says De Fayet.
252 Boulevard Saint-Germain, 75007
+33 (0)1 4325 8791
molli.com

⑥
Alaïa, Le Marais (4^e^)
Couture's national treasure

Azzedine Alaïa's name immediately evokes bodycon dresses, waisted coats and impossibly high heels. The talented couturier created his own line in 1979 and 20 years later moved into a warehouse in Le Marais. The ground floor became this shop selling the brand's latest designs.

The space is filled with interesting artwork: take a peek at the portrait of Alaïa painted by Julian Schnabel in the shop's communal dressing room. If you are in luck, you might spot the designer himself as he lives in the building.
7 Rue de Moussy, 75004
+33 (0)1 4272 1919
alaia.fr

Smell of success

Atelier Cologne's boutiques house worktables, lamps and engraving machines sourced from vintage French and US factories. These spaces set the stage for individual consultations to personalise the leather case of your perfume bottle.
ateliercologne.com

⑦
La Contrie, Tuileries (1^e^)
Custom-made classics

Edwina de Charette was seeking a beautiful and relatively affordable handbag in Paris but couldn't find one – hence her decision to launch La Contrie in 2011. Set in a two-storey space, her shop and atelier brings modernity to a traditional process of craftsmanship.

Customers can choose from a dozen practical and timeless bags and then handpick every single detail – from the type of leather to the lining's colour – according to their taste; additional options include engraving initials into the bag or hemming it with a flashy nautical rope. The basement holds the atelier, which employs five artisans who are on hand to make the chosen bag in about three months. The possibilities are endless; as one of the craftsmen told us, "Anything is possible, as long as it stays close to La Contrie's aesthetic."
11 Rue de la Sourdière, 75001
+33 (0)1 4927 0644
lacontrie.com

Homes and decor
Inside knowledge

①
Astier de Villatte, Louvre (1^e^)
New antiques

Astier de Villatte is known for its imperfect and old-looking ceramics, including plates, cups and teapots. The brand's tiny shop was previously owned by Napoleon Bonaparte's silversmith; inside not much has changed, except it now holds candles, printed notebooks and tableware.

All of the wares are made in Astier de Villatte's factory in the 13th arrondissement. If you happen to visit the shop in December be sure to stop by the first floor, a small room that transforms into a magical Christmas grotto.
173 Rue Saint-Honoré, 75001
+33 (0)1 4260 7413
astierdevillatte.com

2
L'Appartement Red, Le Marais (4e)
Inside job

Only a truly excellent homeware shop can make you contemplate theft and L'Appartement Red certainly ticks the box. The showroom is the work of Parisian design collective Red Edition, whose style takes mid-century Scandinavian cues but is still distinctly French. Kidney-shaped marble coffee tables by UK designer David Hodkinson sit alongside wooden bureau desks by Sabrina Ficarra and a breadth of in-house pieces such as the pleasingly misshapen Eclipse lamp – all set against striking deep-blue walls.
38 Rue des Blancs Manteaux, 75004
+33 (0)1 4337 0287
rededition.com

3
Deyrolle,
Saint-Germain-des-Prés (7e)
Animal house

Deyrolle is as close to a museum as a boutique can be. Founded in 1831, the house settled on the Rue du Bac in a former *hôtel particulier* in 1888. Over a century has passed but the natural-history shop has retained its yesteryear charm.

Taxidermy enthusiasts can spend hours wandering the displays of stuffed animals and framed insects, from birds to bears, beetles to butterflies. With its ancient wooded panels, old moldings and antique display cabinets, the building is a curiosity in itself.
46 Rue du Bac, 75007
+33 (0)1 4222 3007
deyrolle.com

4
India Mahdavi,
Saint-Germain-des-Prés (7e)
Feel-good design

India Mahdavi's signature homeware designs are popular with hoteliers, café owners and interior designers all around the world. After working for Christian Liaigre, the designer opened this showroom; the furniture and objects she makes combine her love of colour, curvaceous shapes and masculine materials. A signature piece is the "Bishop" ceramic stool.

A few doors down, Mahdavi (*pictured*) has another outlet selling her "*Petits Objets*": ashtrays, patchwork cushions, braided chairs and graphic-printed plates.
3 & 19 Rue Las Cases, 75007
+33 (0)1 4555 6767
india-mahdavi.com

Raise a glass

Saint-Louis is the oldest French glass manufacturer: it was established in 1586 and King Louis XV named it a royal glassmaker in 1767. The house continues to produce some of the world's finest glasses, carafes and chandeliers.
saint-louis.com

Specialist retailers
Nice and niche

Carry on
L/Uniform's simple bags have endless appeal

I need a carry bag from L/Uniform

1

L/Uniform,
Saint-Germain-des-Prés (6e)
In the bag

The Paris fashion scene isn't all haute couture and big-name fashion houses. Shaking things up is young bag-maker L/Uniform. Eschewing the idea of super-expensive "it bags", Jeanne Signoles's label opts instead for a simple and functional style in only two materials: woven canvas and leather.

Signoles, a former investment banker and veteran of Goyard (*see page 54*), manufactures the bags in specialist workshops in Carcassonne, a medieval town in the south of France. The brand's compact but beautiful store on the Left Bank was designed by Masamichi Katayama's design firm Wonderwall.

Practicality aside, customisation is the brand's appeal: customers can choose their preferred colourway and have their bag monogrammed.

21 Quai Malaquais, 75006
+33 (0)1 4261 7627
luniform.com

2

Doursoux, Montparnasse (15e)
Military operation

Since 1973, Doursoux has kitted out the French police, army, firemen and custom officers and now it's open to the general public. The shop sells plenty of military jackets, khaki pants and lace-up boots, and also manufactures its own reproductions of classic military uniforms.

It's definitely worth a visit, if only for its endless stock of good basics, including quality Breton shirts and durable leather jackets. Vintage collectors will enjoy the rare finds, including compasses from the Second World War.

3 Passage Alexandre, 75015
+33 (0)1 4327 0097
doursoux.com

Record shops

01 **Big Smile Bazaar, Bonne Nouvelle:** Founded by three vinyl experts, this small shop sells a handpicked selection with a focus on hip-hop, 1980s rock'n'roll and Brazilian sounds.
bigsmilebazaar.com

02 **Nationale 7, Gare du Nord:** Franck Pompidor and Maximin Jacquier are lovers of good music and design. Together they dreamt up this shop where you can go in with the intention of browsing a range of independent vinyl records and find yourself emerging with a piece of mid-century furniture.
nationale7paris.com

03 **L'International Records, Folie-Méricourt:** A slick space with a well-curated selection of vinyl and CDs old and new. It's the work of the owners of bar L'International on the same street, which hosts free gigs throughout the week.
+33 (0)9 8057 1261

(3)

Atelier Green Factory, Canal Saint-Martin (10^{e})

Planting a seed

The idea behind Green Factory came to Noam Levy (*pictured*) when he realised that many people are looking for beautiful plants that don't require much care. His strong knowledge of botany led him to create small and self-sufficient gardens inside glass jars.

"You just have to place your garden near a window, water it a couple of times a year and photosynthesis does the rest," says Levy, who manufactures his terrariums inside his tiny shop near the Canal Saint-Martin.

17 Rue Lucien Sampaix, 75010
+33 (0)1 7464 5615
greenfactory.fr

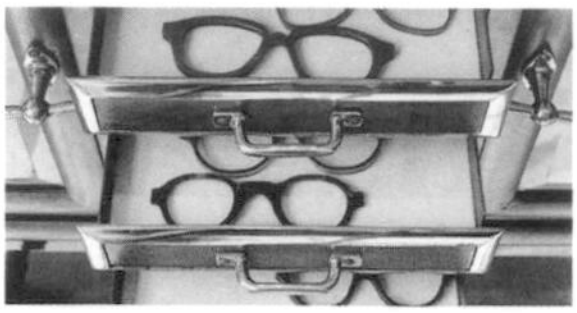

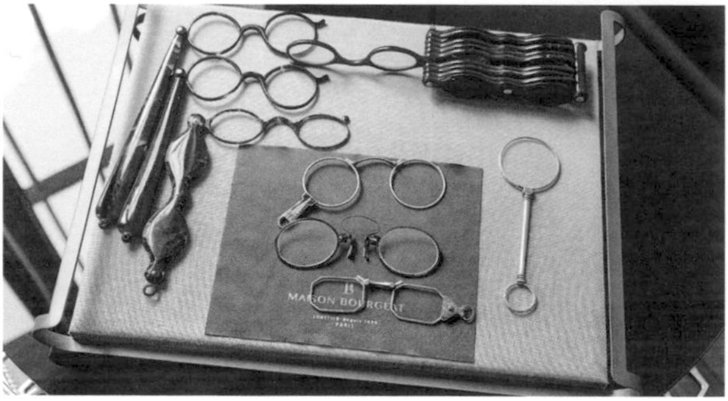

(4)

Maison Bourgeat, Champs-Élysées (8e)

Seeing the bigger picture

This time-honoured French glasses manufacturer has passed from hand to hand and entrepreneur Harry Bessis is the latest to take the helm, with the hope of bringing it into the modern age while preserving its heritage. "I thought that French eyewear-makers had achieved mastery, especially at Maison Bourgeat, which is why I wanted to relaunch the brand," he says.

The 220 styles on offer in the shop-cum-workshop are made to order and take about three weeks; this is precise, scientifically minded craftsmanship at its finest. A smaller sister brand, La Petite Maison Bourgeat, is slated to open soon, offering more affordable models to a wider audience.

134 Rue du Faubourg Saint-Honoré, 75008
+33 (0)1 4289 0571
maisonbourgeat.fr

(5)

Buly 1803, Saint-Germain-des-Prés (6e)

Traditional tinctures

The pharmacy "Bully" was a stalwart of the 19th century. Today l'Officine Universelle Buly has been reborn on Rue Bonaparte with strong references to its rich history. Perfumes infused with bergamot sit next to velvety skin ointments and dental opiates; aged apothecary bottles line the wooden shelves and marbled countertops.

When they are not travelling the world sourcing all-natural ingredients, owners Ramdane Touhami and Victoire de Taillac-Touhami are in the shop explaining each product.

6 Rue Bonaparte, 75006
+33 (0)1 4329 0250
buly1803.com

6
Isaac Reina, Le Marais (3e)
Hide to seek

Hardcore Hermès fans should also make their way to the atelier of Isaac Reina (*pictured*), one-time assistant to the famous brand's art director Véronique Nichanian. His collection of beautiful leather goods includes not only bags and wallets but also toiletry kits and stationery items.

"I like when my items look like they have been designed by no one," Reina says. The Spanish designer studied architecture in Barcelona, where he was inspired by industrial design and mass-market shapes: his creations reflect this approach.
12 Rue de Thorigny, 75003
+33 (0)1 4278 8195
isaacreina.com

7
Bernard Zins,
Saint-Germain-des-Prés (7e)
Strides ahead

Every wardrobe needs at least one pair of immaculately tailored trousers. In this shop, Frank Zins continues the work of his dad Bernard, a tailor who developed a new manufacturing technique for trousers with an adjustable waistband in 1959. Zins trousers still set a standard that the biggest brands try to emulate.

For both men and women who are seeking everything from smart trousers and classy chinos to brightly coloured bermuda shorts, this is undoubtedly the *pantalonnier* to visit.
11 Rue de Luynes, 75007
+33 (0)9 8254 7066
zins.com

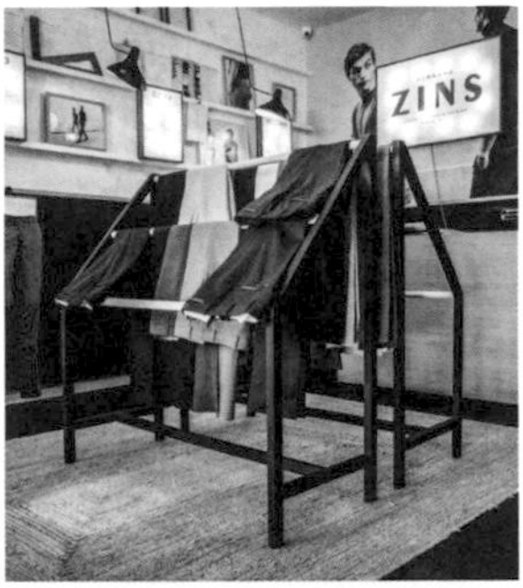

In full bloom

"I have always been fond of flowers," says Karine Garillon, owner of Sol y Flor. Her Rue Madame shop sells fresh roses, tulips, windflowers and ranunculus she brings back from Rungis Market. "I like to have a great deal of flowers in store," the florist adds.
solyflor.fr

Bookshops
Recommended reading

1
Shakespeare and Company,
Latin Quarter (5e)
Your bard

"Everyone who comes here should feel they inherited a bookshop on the Seine," says owner Sylvia Beach Whitman; she's named after Sylvia Beach, who founded the original Shakespeare and Company bookshop in 1919. Sylvia Whitman's father, George, opened this version a stone's throw from Notre-Dame in 1951.

The first shop became strongly associated with the writers of the Lost Generation and this reincarnation hosted the authors of the Beat Generation. Sylvia has embraced the tradition of housing young resident writers – otherwise known as "tumbleweeds" – who rub shoulders with students and ex-pats browsing the labyrinthine shelves. "It's an Anglophone island in Paris," says Sylvia. "I wouldn't want to be anywhere else."
37 Rue de la Bûcherie, 75005
+33 (0)1 4325 4093
shakespeareandcompany.com

Stacked up — 7L stocks all manner of rare titles and publishers

Antiques
Old ones are the best

② 7L, Saint-Germain-des-Prés (7e)
On-trend titles

At the cultural crossroads of Paris between the Musée d'Orsay, the Louvre and Saint-Germain-des-Près sits Karl Lagerfeld's exquisitely curated bookshop. The books lining the shelves hold titles on subjects ranging from art and design to landscape photography.

"We try to build bridges between the different themes and subjects," says co-manager Hervé Le Masson. Lagerfeld visits frequently, often recommending books for the shop: "'Oh, I saw this book, you must have it,' he'll say," adds Le Masson.
7 Rue de Lille, 75007
+33 (0)1 4292 0358
librairie7l.com

③ Galignani, Tuileries (1e)
Treasured tomes

A stone plaque by the entrance to this independent institution reads, "The first English bookshop established on the continent". Run by six generations of the Galignani family, it has been a must-visit for Parisians and visitors seeking English titles since 1801.

Wooden bookshelves adorned with busts of literary figures stock tens of thousands of books. They are accessible by wooden ladders that slide along a brass rail; from the top you get great views of the stucco ceiling and glass roof.
224 Rue de Rivoli, 75001
+33 (0)1 4260 7607
galignani.fr

④ Booksellers on the Seine
Priceless find

Even in the rain the *bouquinistes* of Paris unlock the hatches of their green wooden bookstalls that have lined the banks of the Seine for centuries. The stalls stretch for about 2.5km along the Left Bank. The Unesco World Heritage site is home to more than 300,000 books from rare volumes by Jules Vernes to vintage magazines.

① Florence Lopez, Saint-Germain-des-Prés (6e)
Open house

Florence Lopez, who likes to describe herself as both an antiquarian and a scenographer, started selling early 20th-century pieces after working with renowned decorators such as Jacques Garcia. "About 20 years ago I bought this apartment and started using it as a space to showcase what I do," she says.

Over time she began decorating houses for her numerous clients – Charlotte Gainsbourg and Yvan Attal among them – in line with her eclectic taste. Lopez's place, where she receives guests by appointment, reflects her eye for bold colour palettes and her love of US and Brazilian designers. "This place has been with me since the beginning; it feels great to think that it witnessed my style's evolution from the start."
18 Rue du Dragon, 75006
+33 (0)6 6044 3375
florencelopez.com

②

Maison Nordik, Montmartre (18e)

Northern soul

Designers Gregory Donatien (*pictured*) and Louise Vyff decided to share their love for vintage Scandinavian furniture by opening this shop on the quiet Rue Marcadet in 2013. Set on two levels, the space features the best design that northern Europe has to offer, collected by Vyff's parents on frequent trips to Norway, Denmark and Sweden, hunting for 1950s desks, tables and commodes.

"A loaded truck comes in every month so everything changes regularly," says Vyff. "People often wonder if the merchandise is new because we restore and polish every piece of furniture before selling it." The couple also stocks a range of modern design objects for the home, including candle-holders and blankets.

159 Rue Marcadet, 75018
+33 (0)1 622 072 107
maisonnordik.com

When packing an antique it pays to be thorough

Art and antiques galleries

01 **Galerie Pascal Cuisinier, Saint-Germain-des-Prés:** An expert on early French designers, Pascal Cuisinier opened his gallery in 2006, where he shows rare pieces made between 1951 and 1961. Functional and innovative furniture from Pierre Paulin, Joseph-André Motte and Michel Mortier are all part of his selection.
galeriepascalcuisinier.com

02 **Galerie Richard, Le Marais:** With an exhibition space consisting of four rooms, Jean-Luc and Takako Richard's gallery is the place to discover emerging 21st-century painters. Indeed, the husband-and-wife team were the first to represent new talents such as Adam Ross, Kiyoshi Nagakami and David Ryan in Europe.
galerierichard.com

03 **Galerie Patrick Seguin, Bastille:** Azzedine Alaïa, Ronald Lauder and Peter Brant are just a few of the collectors who come to Seguin's space in the Bastille district. The gallery, designed by Jean Nouvel, specialises in Jean Prouvé's work and holds the most impressive collection of his prefab houses.
patrickseguin.com

04 **Galerie Downtown, Saint-Germain-des-Prés:** An early Prouvé collector, François Laffanour opened his own gallery in the early 1980s after selling at the Marché aux Puces de Saint-Ouen market. He quickly became a familiar sight at contemporary art and design fairs but he still shows Le Corbusier and Charlotte Perriand pieces here.
galeriedowntown.com

③
Galerie Jacques Lacoste, Saint-Germain-des-Prés (6e)
20th-century treasures

The ultimate Jean Royère specialist, Lacoste is passionate about furniture and objects dating from 1930 to 1950; his space features rare pieces from designers such as Charlotte Perriand and Alexandre Noll.

The secret to his collection lies in the fact that he sources first editions by tracking them to their current owners. Design enthusiasts know they can come here for that Royère chair they have been dreaming of – unless Lacoste has decided to keep it for himself.
12 Rue de Seine, 75006
+33 (0)1 4020 4182
jacqueslacoste.fr

Flea markets
Blissful browsing

①
Marché aux Fleurs, Île de la Cité (4e)
Birds and bees

This picturesque market was founded on the Île de la Cité in 1808 and consists of flowers, trees and essential gardening tools; make sure to stop by La Maison de l'Orchidée for its wonderful orchids. On Sunday, the *marché* turns into a bird market.
Place Louis Lépine et Quai de la Corse, 75004

TOP STALLS
01 Stéphanie has the biggest choice of flowers and small trees.
02 Vertige sells everything from tiny plants to candle-holders.
03 Maison Meunier has all kinds of interior decorations.

Sew special

Entering La Droguerie, a haberdashery shop that has been standing in Les Halles since 1975, is like stepping into Ali Baba's cave. You can't help but be amazed by the array of vegetable dyes, glitter, beads and buttons.
ladroguerie.com

②
Marché aux Puces de Vanves, Porte de Vanves (14e)
Shared passion

This flea market has been around since the end of the 19th century. Every Saturday and Sunday you'll find antiquarians setting up their stalls to display trinkets, books, furniture and vintage clothing.

Julia Staudemmann's stall, found at 167 Avenue Marc Sangnier, is a must-see: she has been selling retro advertising, children's games and one-of-a-kind objects for 14 years. "Les Puces de Vanves is a great place to meet new, interesting and passionate people," she says. "I couldn't imagine selling my antiques anywhere else."
Avenues Marc Sangnier et Georges Lafenestre, 75014

TOP STALLS
01 Martine Archambault specialises in silverware.
02 Dominique Govelet's vinyls and vintage record players are a delight.
03 Martine Dudek sells countless buttons, pearls and linens.

Yes, I always bring my own trolley to the marché

Keep fit

The Saint-Ouen market covers seven hectares

3

Marché aux Puces de Saint-Ouen, Saint-Ouen (18e)
Stroll through history

The Marché aux Puces de Saint-Ouen was founded in 1885. With more than 2,000 stalls to explore, this flea market is a treasure trove of furniture, precious jewellery and second-hand clothing. True collectors always stop by the Paul Bert Serpette market for its exquisite selection of rare antiques.

Another popular pit-stop is the Philippe Starck-designed Ma Cocotte restaurant, which has typical French dishes on the menu (*see page 32*). The market recently welcomed Habitat 1964, a space dedicated to buying and selling original vintage furniture from British brand Habitat. Keep in mind that it's only open at the weekend and Mondays.
Avenue de la Porte de Clignancourt, 75018

TOP STALLS

01 At Le Monde du Voyage, Alain Zisul sells restored Hermès, Goyard and Louis Vuitton trunks.
02 Chez Sarah, the market's biggest vintage clothing shop, offers pieces dating from 1880 to 1980.
03 Vintagez-Vous opened in early 2013 and specialises in furniture from 1950 to 1970.

Things we'd buy
— Parisian purchases

It's hard to bid *au revoir* to the French capital without stuffing a substantial hoard from the country's leading luxury brands into your suitcase. We recommend starting with Dior fragrances, Chanel cosmetics and the Parisian classic – a Saint Laurent beret. In line with tradition a bold bottle of red should also make it onto your list, along with some crystal glassware by one of the country's longest-standing glass-manufacturers Saint-Louis. And don't put away your credit card just yet: there's a rising wave of young and independent brands to buy from, such as L/Uniform with its range of woven-canvas-and-leather bags and Maison Kitsuné – who could resist that genteel menswear collection?

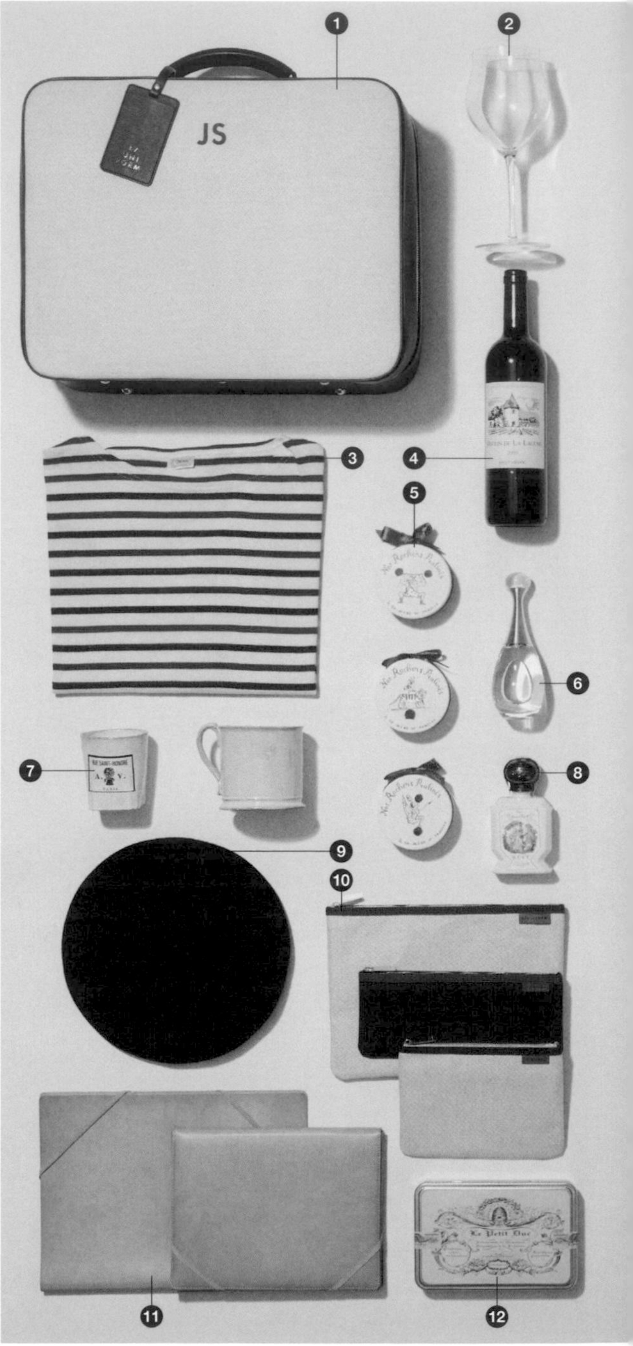

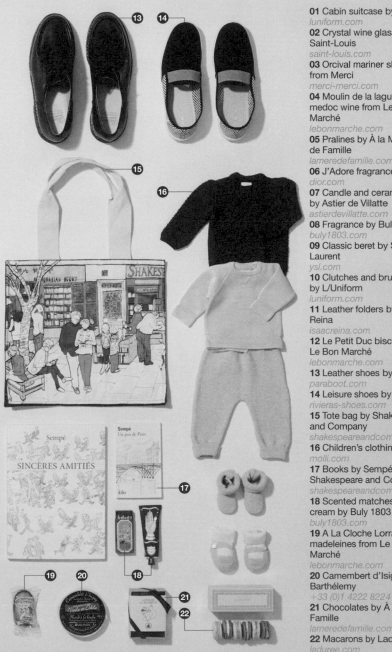

01 Cabin suitcase by L/Uniform
luniform.com
02 Crystal wine glasses by Saint-Louis
saint-louis.com
03 Orcival mariner shirt from Merci
merci-merci.com
04 Moulin de la lagune haut-medoc wine from Le Bon Marché
lebonmarche.com
05 Pralines by À la Mère de Famille
lameredefamille.com
06 J'Adore fragrance by Dior
dior.com
07 Candle and ceramic cup by Astier de Villatte
astierdevillatte.com
08 Fragrance by Buly 1803
buly1803.com
09 Classic beret by Saint Laurent
ysl.com
10 Clutches and brush pouch by L/Uniform
luniform.com
11 Leather folders by Isaac Reina
isaacreina.com
12 Le Petit Duc biscuits from Le Bon Marché
lebonmarche.com
13 Leather shoes by Paraboot
paraboot.com
14 Leisure shoes by Rivieras
rivieras-shoes.com
15 Tote bag by Shakespeare and Company
shakespeareandcompany.com
16 Children's clothing by Molli
molli.com
17 Books by Sempé from Shakespeare and Company
shakespeareandcompany.com
18 Scented matches and hand cream by Buly 1803
buly1803.com
19 A La Cloche Lorraine madeleines from Le Bon Marché
lebonmarche.com
20 Camembert d'Isigny from Barthélemy
+33 (0)1 4222 8224
21 Chocolates by À la Mère de Famille
lameredefamille.com
22 Macarons by Ladurée
laduree.com

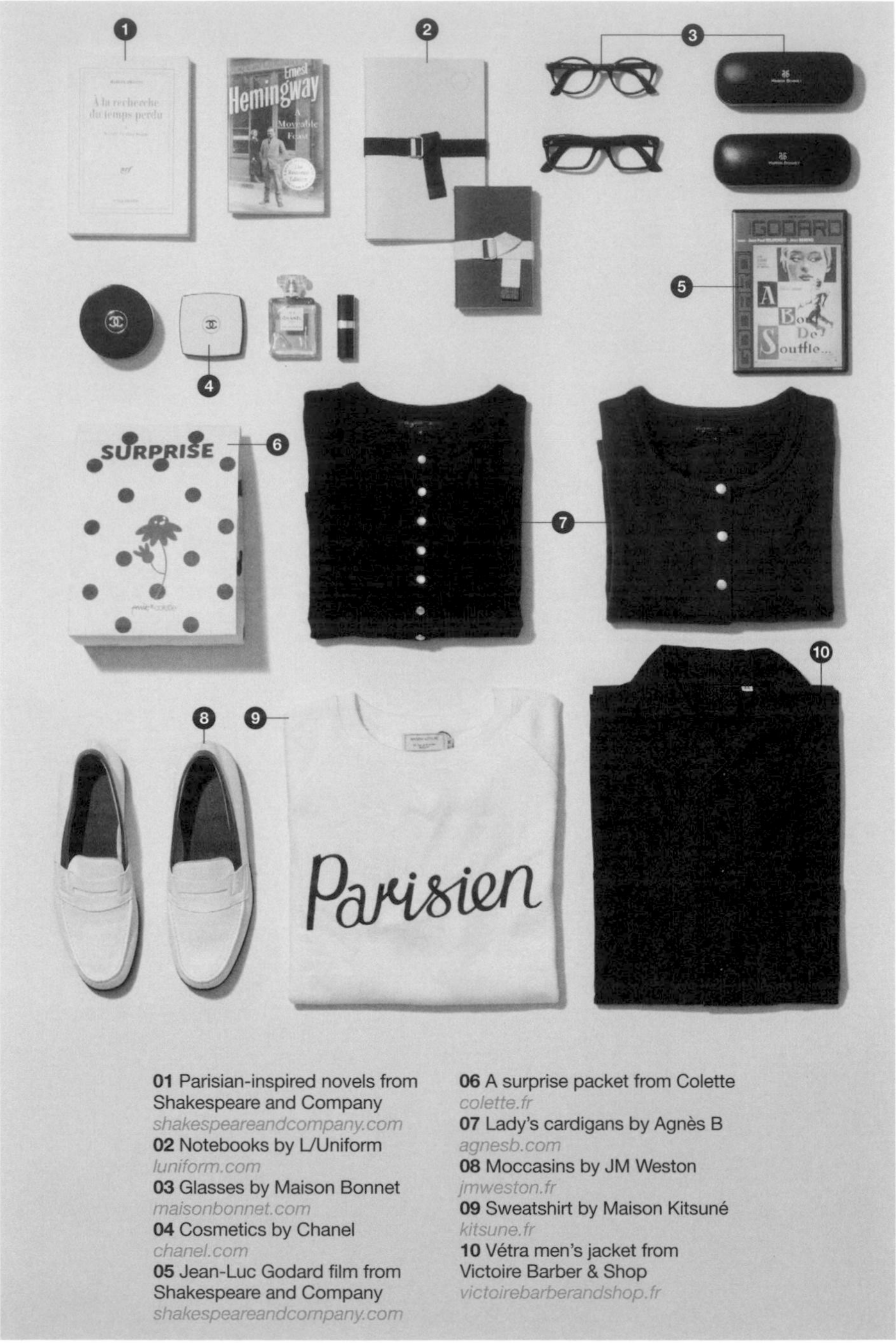

01 Parisian-inspired novels from Shakespeare and Company
shakespeareandcompany.com
02 Notebooks by L/Uniform
luniform.com
03 Glasses by Maison Bonnet
maisonbonnet.com
04 Cosmetics by Chanel
chanel.com
05 Jean-Luc Godard film from Shakespeare and Company
shakespeareandcompany.com
06 A surprise packet from Colette
colette.fr
07 Lady's cardigans by Agnès B
agnesb.com
08 Moccasins by JM Weston
jmweston.fr
09 Sweatshirt by Maison Kitsuné
kitsune.fr
10 Vétra men's jacket from Victoire Barber & Shop
victoirebarberandshop.fr

12 essays
— Paris uncovered

Kant tear myself away from this fascinating guide...

ESSAY 01

Ms Piaf's table

Cultural roots of the city

For all of Paris's vibrancy, its story is best evoked in the places where time just marched on past. To find them you'll have to take the 'rue' less travelled – just like the artists and thinkers who made the city famous.

by Margault Antonini, journalist

There are plenty of ways to get to know Paris. You could hop on one of the buses that funnel people to the most renowned – and somewhat predictable – spots. Or you might decide to have a wander in a hip, probably crowded, neighbourhood in the hope of stumbling upon some unspoilt trace of the old city. Take a longer stroll and you may even find echoes of a former *malletier*, pass the building where writers Louis Aragon and Elsa Triolet used to live or end up in a park sitting beneath Françoise Hardy's favourite tree.

Paris is forward-looking and dynamic but it's also a place with a rich heritage and some things have, thankfully, remained unchanged. The recent overhaul of the famous Pont des Arts reveals that citizens care enough about the city's history to make sure modernity doesn't mean saying goodbye to their most treasured places. True Parisians are picky when it comes to change; they don't always cheer a faddish new opening if it lacks the authenticity and charm of the rest of their neighbourhood.

> *"In many districts the places that made the city's reputation are still around"*

Thankfully, Paris is good at telling its own story and signs everywhere remind visitors that even the most insignificant street corner, bench or public garden has its own tale to share. In many districts the places that made the city's reputation are still around, such as in Saint-Germain-des-Prés where, after the Second World War, cafés and nightclubs buzzed with writers, artists and musicians. Gathering to dance to American jazz in basements or discuss existentialism on pavement terraces, they gave the neighbourhood a village atmosphere; Simone de Beauvoir could be found here and her lover and fellow philosopher Jean-Paul Sartre was often spotted at the Café de Flore. There he would work or talk with other writers, sometimes until late at night while ordering no more than a single cup of coffee. He also had a habit of picking up customers' discarded cigarette butts to fill his pipe, to the despair of the Flore's owner.

Not far away, cinephiles could be found in independent picture house Le Champo, which showed its first film in 1938. It became a hub for the film-makers who transformed French cinema in the 1950s and 1960s; François Truffaut called the art deco building his "headquarters" and Claude Chabrol dubbed the cinema his "second university". It still screens old movies and classics to an in-the-know band of insiders.

Intellectuals and creatives of every stripe mingled at La Closerie des Lilas, a typical French brasserie built in the early 19th century. Between the wars it became an unofficial meeting point for Americans in Paris – take a spot on the terrace and you'll be sitting where, it's said, F Scott Fitzgerald showed Ernest Hemingway his first draft of *The Great Gatsby*. Hemingway

Favourite meeting places

01 Harry's Bar, Opéra
The birthplace of many world-famous cocktails.
02 Le Procope, Odéon
A café that's been around since the 17th century.
03 Angelina's, Tuileries
The best homemade hot chocolate in town.

later recalled how he wrote here too, completing his first novel *The Sun Also Rises* in just six weeks at one of the café's tables.

Any afternoon is perfect for a dive into Parisian culture away from the usual museum trail. The city is blessed with a host of small, relatively unknown treasure troves, such as the collection of Bernard Marchois, a lifelong admirer of Édith Piaf. The memorabilia he has amassed over 50 years about Piaf is the core of a museum he set up in his apartment, tucked away in the Ménilmontant neighbourhood. Among the many objects on show are dozens of pictures, letters from Piaf to her half-sister Denise, the boxing gloves that belonged to her lover Marcel Cerdan and even the black dresses she wore while performing. Visits are by appointment but it's worth the effort – just ask the owner about his encounter with La Môme in 1958 and he will be delighted to tell you all about it. For more of Piaf's Paris, stop off in the Strasbourg Saint-Denis area; the Brasserie Julien, a true art nouveau wonder, is where she used to wait while Cerdan sparred in his gym nearby. If you're in luck, you might be seated at table 24, Piaf's favourite perch.

No tour of Paris would be complete without dinner but Maxim's is the only destination where the city's love of food truly comes together with its cultural heritage. Owned by designer Pierre Cardin, the restaurant boasts an exceptional private collection of rare art nouveau pieces housed across several floors above the dining rooms. During the 1930s Maxim's became one of the world's most prestigious gastronomic names and was later a favourite of Jean Cocteau and his partner Jean Marais during German occupation. After the war, Maria Callas could be found here with her lover Aristotle Onassis, sometimes joined by Marlene Dietrich.

If sampling Paris's nightlife seems the perfect way to round off the day, recently reopened Chez Castel is a must. Its golden era was during the 1970s when it was frequented by every one of the city's famous residents, including actresses Romy Schneider and Catherine Deneuve. Tucked down a small street in the 6th arrondissement, it was Serge Gainsbourg's favourite nightclub (his piano still sits in the *fumoir* downstairs) and was Princess Caroline of Monaco's place of choice to dance the night away. Just be aware that a tasteful outfit is still *de rigueur* whoever you are; Mick Jagger was turned away for turning up in jeans. And that's another thing that hasn't changed: Parisians may like to make everything seem effortless but they always enjoy looking good. — (M)

i

ABOUT THE WRITER: Margault Antonini is a freelance journalist and co-founder of editorial agency Les Dactylos. A Paris native, she never tires of wandering around the city, especially if a museum visit is on the cards.

ESSAY 02

Projecting Paris
The city on screen

The City of Lights is a fitting birthplace for cinema and, growing up alongside the luminous art form, it became something of a screen idol itself. Take a wander through the streets of Paris and you'll find its most famous scenes are still set. Ready for your close-up?

by Eugenia Ellanskaya, writer

Paris is where cinema was born: the Lumière brothers' unveiling of the *cinématographe* camera in 1895 heralded the first public film screening in history. Since then, the city itself has become a film star and a character in its own right, providing the iconic backdrop to more than 1,500 movies that simply wouldn't be the same – or exist at all – if they had been played out in any other city.

Take *Amélie* (2001), for example. Many cinemagoers' expectations of what a French film, and Paris in particular, looks and sounds like are defined by Jean-Pierre Jeunet's glossy, whimsical and very exportable tale. Its global appeal is such that it sparked cinephile pilgrimages to the city's 18th arrondissement: the picturesque Lamarck-Caulaincourt metro station where Amélie (Audrey Tautou) escorts a blind tramp across the streets and whispers all the things he cannot see into his ear; the humble grocer's Au Marché de la Butte ("Maison Colignon fondée 1956" in the film), one metro stop down at Abbesses where Amélie does her shopping and where the real shopkeeper is only too happy to indulge in Amélie-related chit-chat; and the low-key Café des Deux Moulins where Amélie works is also nearby.

Then there's the Latin Quarter of Woody Allen's 2011 romantic comedy *Midnight in Paris*. As flawed as a guide as it is as a film, it nevertheless captures the magical atmosphere of this neighbourhood in which Owen Wilson's character Gil gets lost in time night after night. Take a break on the steps of the Saint-Étienne-du-Mont church that's snuggled behind the Panthéon (preferably at about midnight) and you might feel that you too could be whisked off for an adventure in 1920s Paris. Gil must at least be applauded for his more tangible pursuit of the photogenic Shakespeare and Company bookshop, located in the 5th arrondissement facing Notre Dame Cathedral. Once the haunt of bohemian authors, it's also where Ethan Hawke and Julie Delpy reunite in Richard Linklater's *Before Sunset*. Come here for author Q&As, English-language literary clubs or just to hang out upstairs listening to an impromptu piano performance.

Paris as big screen's picture-perfect city isn't a modern development, however. The Moulin Rouge of Jean Renoir's 1955 musical *French Cancan* contrasts sharply with the gritty 9th arrondissement of François Truffaut's 1959 *The 400 Blows*. Truffaut's New Wave classic traces the life of a young boy as he gets caught in a downward spiral of petty crime. His experimental coming-of-age tale is a warts-and-all picture of Paris but one that won Truffaut the best director award at Cannes in 1959.

> *"Paris has been the backdrop to more than 1,500 movies that simply wouldn't be the same – or exist at all – if they had been played out in any other city"*

Cinema's love affair with Paris often centres on Monsieur Eiffel's construction, built for the Exposition Universelle in 1889. It's been a prop on most Paris-set films ever since, although not all creative Parisians have been so enamoured with it: Guy de Maupassant hated the Eiffel Tower so much he dined at its restaurant every day – the only place where he couldn't see it. The 1995 drama *La Haine* also cast a critical gaze on the landmark: not the eyes of lovers on a leisurely stroll but of disaffected youth from the *banlieue* complaining that they can't switch off its lights. Writer-director Mathieu Kassovitz captures 24 hours in the racially charged reality of the streets, with the anti-heroes rolling to an audacious mix of Édith Piaf's "Non, je ne regrette rien" and the gangster rap of "Assassin de la police".

France has the most successful film industry in Europe, both in the number of films produced annually and the number of titles exported. Paris in particular has been a fertile ground, both as a setting for some of the most influential films ever made and as an inspiration for cinéastes the world over. Cinema just cannot get enough of the place. — (M)

Cinematic landmarks

—

01 Salon Indien du Grand Café
The original venue of the first public cinema screening.
02 Cinémathèque Française
One of the largest archives of films and film-related objects in the world.
03 Le Champo
An independent cinema in the Latin Quarter.

i

ABOUT THE WRITER: Eugenia Ellanskaya was born in Moscow and grew up in London. She became infatuated with French cinema at a young age thanks to the mysterious popularity of 1970s French comedies on Russian television.

ESSAY 03

Lucky 13
My secret Paris

Beyond the tourist-thronged centre, the city's edgier arrondissements are well worth a visit. The 13th, for example, with its picturesque lanes, street art and radical chic has a growing coterie of fans to speak up for its charms.

by Heather Stimmler-Hall, author

After apartment-hopping all over Paris since moving here in 1995, I've made the 13th arrondissement my home and, like any local, I'm convinced my neighbourhood is the most authentically Parisian. "Isn't that Chinatown?" ask those who rarely venture east of the Latin Quarter. And yes, the 13th is home to the largest Chinatown in Europe but that's just one of the half-dozen neighbourhoods that make up this diverse area.

Visitors often ask me to show them parts of the city they'd never discover on their own. If it's hard to convince Parisians to visit the 13th, imagine how hard it is to convince tourists, but this vast district bordering the 5th arrondissement and the Seine is both typically Parisian in its charming neighbourhoods and home to a striking blend of cutting-edge modern architecture and riverside entertainment.

I ease newcomers in by starting in my own district on the tree-lined Avenue des Gobelins. This part of the 13th is known for its Haussmann-era residences, Louis XIV's 17th-century Manufacture des Gobelins tapestry workshop and the prestigious École Estienne art school, where photojournalism pioneer Robert Doisneau studied in the 1920s. Its cinemas include Les Fauvettes, which shows digitally remastered classics and the silent-film temple of Fondation Seydoux-Pathé, with a façade sculpted by Rodin and an interior completely rebuilt by architect Renzo Piano in 2014. There are plenty of low-key cafés, shops and restaurants catering to locals, as well as a huge open-air food market three mornings a week along the Boulevard Auguste Blanqui, stretching from Place d'Italie to the Metro Corvisart.

From there, I like to take a slow climb up to the Buttes-aux-Cailles, a hillside spot where terraced houses with wisteria vines line cobblestone streets. A natural spring provides drinking water for the locals and fills the art deco municipal swimming pool, recently restored to its former glory. The budget bistros and inexpensive bars lining Rue de la Butte aux Cailles and Rue des Cinq Diamants are popular with students and the area's radical heritage is much in evidence. Neighbourhood restaurant Le Temps des Cerises is a workers' co-operative named after a revolutionary song, while the historic society Les Amis de la Commune de Paris reminds visitors that this hill was once a stronghold of the city's bloody civil uprising in 1871. Today the locals' lefty leanings usually manifest themselves in nothing more than cheeky street art by

Best meals in the 13th

01 Butte aux Piafs
A relaxed bistro overlooking the Auguste Blanqui market.

02 Tempero
French fusion cuisine and the best-value lunch menu in town.

03 La Dame du Canton
Dine in the cosy captain's lair of this pirate ship.

> *"Most Parisians still need convincing that the 13th is not some obscure suburb but a part of Paris worthy of their attention"*

renowned Parisian graffiti artists such as MissTic and Jef Aerosol.

This cityscape is a far cry from the days when the 13th was an assortment of villages, annexed to Paris in 1860 under Napoleon III's Second Empire. They morphed into poor working-class districts, their ancient tanneries and breweries replaced by turn-of-the-century mills and manufacturing plants, including the city's first automobile factory. The first wave of redevelopment in the 1960s brought modern high rises, including the first residential tower, La Tour Albert. Also known as Gratte Ciel #1, it was completed in 1960 to give Parisians what *Le Figaro* called "a home in the clouds high above the noisy city".

The buildings on the Butte are rarely more than four storeys tall – the ground below is riddled with old quarry tunnels – and the view to the east is dominated by ugly towers. But if you know where to look, you'll find that entire terraced streets of adorable houses built for factory workers in the early 1900s somehow escaped demolition, such as the Square des Peupliers and the Rue Ernest et Henri Rousselle. Today these homes with their private gardens are highly coveted.

Once I've convinced my visitors of the 13th's hidden charms, I show them something completely different. The elevated Metro Line 6 takes you through the concrete jungle, where you can see a few examples of the enormous murals covering the façades of old buildings by graffiti artists such as Shepard Fairey (of Obey clothing fame), a trend helped by the mayor of the 13th, who has made it part of his mission to turn this arrondissement into a canvas for street artists from around the world. If you continue to the Quai de la Gare station you'll discover the new Paris Rive Gauche neighbourhood, where the mistakes of the 1960s were avoided in one of the most ambitious redevelopment feats of the past 20 years. Once an industrial wasteland of warehouses and freight train tracks, you can now take the tramway or the driverless Metro Line 14 to reach its mix of offices, homes, shops and cafés, as well as a university campus set amid green spaces and bicycle lanes. A few of the 1920s industrial buildings have been repurposed, such as Les Frigos, a former artists' squat in a refrigerated storehouse officially transformed into artist studios in the 1990s.

Contemporary architecture doesn't impress everyone but few can resist the lure of the Seine, so I always save the quays of the 13th for my finale. This is where some of the most popular entertainment and nightlife venues in Paris can be found on floating bars, cafés and nightclubs on boats moored year-round from the Pont Tolbiac to the Pont Austerlitz. In the summer this place is home to open-air restaurants, live music and even a floating swimming pool. Les Docks (Cité de la Mode et du Design, *see page 117*), the only building in Paris sitting right on the edge of the water, houses a fashion-and-design school, two rooftop restaurants, a nightclub and a brunch spot with wooden decks overlooking the river.

Notre Dame Cathedral is only a 10-minute walk from Les Docks but the cheekily named Off-Paris Seine – a floating hotel moored at Quai d'Austerlitz – implies that even Parisians need convincing that the 13th is not some obscure suburb but a part of Paris worthy of their attention. Judging by the reaction of my visitors, I'm confident the 13th is more than ready to impress even the most sceptical. The only question is, am I willing to share it with them? — (M)

i

ABOUT THE WRITER: Heather Stimmler-Hall is a private tour guide, guidebook author and editor of the *Secrets of Paris* newsletter. Her favourite way to explore the city is on her morning marathon-training runs.

ESSAY 04

Seeing and being seen

A flâneur's Paris

It's hard to think of anywhere other than Paris where the art of simply observing street life would be so valued. Here it's a subculture, an intellectual pursuit and an artistic contribution to the life of the city. And, if you'll put away your devices, it's easy to do. Let's go for a walk.

by Chloë Ashby, Monocle

The first thing you need to learn when you come to Paris is the word flâneur. Then you need to learn how to be one, how to lounge around looking lazy with your eyes fixed on the secret heart of the city.

Paris is a place to see and be seen. With its grand tree-lined boulevards, glowing streetlights and café culture on every corner (it's less about the coffee than the ambience), the city is a people-watcher's paradise. Parisians are notoriously glamorous and wonderfully animated talkers. They can turn lighting a girlfriend's cigarette into a gripping soap opera.

Up until the mid-19th century the city was crowded, its medieval streets meandering and muddy, riddled with congestion and disease after a period of rapid growth. Then came Baron Georges-Eugène Haussmann, the king of creative destruction who dreamed up the postcard city we know today. Commissioned by Napoleon III, he set about clearing space by evicting inhabitants, demolishing unsanitary neighbourhoods and realigning the layout of the districts to create broad vistas. Some critics called the plan – and the man behind it – insane. In the end he created about 135km of new roads, revamped the drainage and sewage systems and brought in streetlights and wide pavements.

Something spectacular rose from the rubble: Haussmann's boulevards cut through the chaos and let in the light. He lifted the curtains and revealed a floodlit stage. Enter the flâneur. Paris

The artist as flâneur

01 **Constantin Guys**
Baudelaire's main man, the king of social observation.
02 **Edgar Degas**
A stroller who chanced upon subjects on the boulevards.
03 **Gustave Caillebotte**
Keen chronicler of urban life and the bourgeoisie.

became the backdrop for the character first described by French poet Charles Baudelaire in his essay *The Painter of Modern Life* (1863). Part observer, part philosopher – "call him what you will", Baudelaire shrugged – the flâneur was a passionate man of leisure whose only ambition was to stroll through the city and scope the crowd. His standard operating procedure: "To see the world, to be at the centre of the world and yet to remain hidden from the world."

"Parisians are wonderfully animated talkers. They can turn lighting a girlfriend's cigarette into a gripping soap opera"

Hidden in plain sight. If sitting at a table without a book, a phone or a laptop sounds disconcerting, don't worry: cafés in the French capital are designed for flying solo. From the intimate Café de Flore, one of the oldest and most venerable observation points in the city, to the bustling Café de la Paix on the Place de l'Opéra, there's a perch for every taste, with each seat facing out onto the street. Every café in Paris comes with a view.

Sometimes there's even an indoor view. Think of the Édouard Manet painting "A Bar at the Folies-Bergère" (1882), that famous image of the barmaid standing in front of a vast mirror reflecting a crowd mingling in a gaslit interior. Manet was one of Baudelaire's protégés and arguably the most accomplished painter of late 19th-century Paris and Parisians. In this painting he perfectly captures the flâneur's world. If you stand in front of this canvas in the Courtauld Gallery at Somerset House in London, you will feel as if you have been transported back to that night at the Folies-Bergère, waiting to be served a drink by the blushing barmaid in the tightly buttoned, lace-trimmed bodice. Between the two of you is a marble counter; behind her the all-important mirror.

"We might liken him to a mirror as vast as the crowd itself," says Baudelaire of the flâneur. Manet surely agreed. In one corner of the mirror a pair of legs balances on a trapeze, a reminder that the Folies-Bergère was a cabaret with light entertainment – that night it was gymnastics. But the mirror also reveals a more conventional spectacle. To the right of the barmaid's reflection we see a mustachioed man in a top hat, staring intently into her eyes. The staff at this popular establishment were hired for their looks and encouraged to flirt in exchange for tips. So are the pair indulging in a private tête-à-tête? Is Manet's skewiff reflection of the barmaid leaning eagerly forward just the top-hatted gentleman's sexual fantasy? After all, what we see is the barmaid standing bolt upright. Maybe we're missing the point. Is the barmaid's dazed and detached expression a symptom of the lonely flâneur's secret alienation?

The mystery of Manet's barmaid, and the mystery of the flâneur, is like the mystery of the passersby on a Paris boulevard. And that's part of the fun. Paris is a theatrical playground crowded with performers, a spectacle arranged for your pleasure. So in an age when sitting or standing perfectly still fills many of us with horror, challenge yourself: put away your props, pull up a pew at one of the city's innumerable cafés and simply observe.

And when you're done, ask for *l'addition*, get up from your seat and take a stroll, joining the cast of the next performance. — (M)

i

ABOUT THE WRITER: Chloë Ashby, associate editor of MONOCLE books, has previously written about art for *The Daily Beast* and *The New York Observer*. A graduate of the Courtauld Institute, she has spent way too much time gazing at Manet's "Bar at the Folies-Bergère" – without anyone noticing her, of course.

ESSAY 05

Stay classic
How to be Parisienne

Take a look at any womenswear collection on any runway and, wherever its designer hails from, its DNA will be French – because Paris invented fashion. But while anyone can buy into Parisienne chic, can anyone but a Frenchwoman truly pull it off?

by Sonia Zhuravlyova, Monocle

It's a truth universally acknowledged: French women have style down to a tee. No stray hairs for them. No mismatched outfits. A scarf tied just so. Big sunglasses; small dog. But is it, in fact, a fact? Or is it the enduring cliché of our time, a projection of our own desires and something that can be marketed and aspired to by millions?

The idea of French chic and timeless allure is endlessly recycled by a world of glossy magazines. "Why are French women so damn cool?" they regularly ask. Why indeed? Yes we can wear what the French wear but can we carry it off like natives of the country that gave us the Breton stripe and Coco Chanel? But however much we embrace the stripe, spritz ourselves with Chanel's signature scent and don pearls, it seems that anyone who is not French just cannot fake it.

The notion of French women's allure, according to Aileen Ribeiro of the Courtauld Institute of Art, is linked to history and national attitudes. It all began with the lavish court of Louis XIV and the spread of luxury goods such as fine silks. The court at Versailles set the standards for the rest of Europe in terms of lifestyle and fashion. Dressing fashionably became a novelty that was constantly changing, communicated by the regular appearance of fashion plates from the 1670s onwards.

"In England the response to fashion was coloured by attitudes towards the French that were informed by wars and growing colonial rivalries," says Ribeiro. "There was a preference to err on the side of comfort and relative simplicity in the years approaching the French Revolution." English women admired and envied French fashion (as did elite women all over Europe) but at the same time they began to value practicality in dress, opting for fabrics such as cotton, a trend that led to the Industrial Revolution.

According to Ribeiro, contemporary literature shows that even then, French women were admired not just for their fashion but also for the manner in which they wore their clothes and how a sense of *esprit* could be felt in their appearance and manners. But at the same time there was a conflicting feeling among their more uptight Anglo-Saxon sisters that fashion is something inherently frivolous and indulgent.

It comes as no surprise then that the first great couturier, Charles Frederick Worth, felt the need to leave London for Paris in 1845. Starting out as a draper's assistant, he soon began designing dresses and finally gained an audience with Empress Eugénie, who became his patron. Where royalty went, moneyed society followed. The House of Worth was among the very first to use live models to show designs, and he was also the first to sew labels into his outfits. He revolutionised the dressmaking system, which was the domain of seamstresses who created one-off pieces for their clients. The flamboyant Worth not only elevated the profession so that the dressmaker could now influence the taste of society but he also created seasonal collections. "Before Worth, the idea of a dress being recognisably the work of its creator didn't exist," says fashion historian Caroline Rennolds Milbank.

> *"A desire to appear clever before appearing beautiful is what's really at the heart of style"*

Fashion icons

01 Coco Chanel
Coco's relaxed designs started a revolution in the fashion world.

02 Catherine Deneuve
Deneuve's classic style is the epitome of Parisian chic.

03 Jean-Paul Gaultier
He's been subverting gender stereotypes in fashion since the early 1980s.

I suspect that today, French women's monopoly on elegance, if it ever really existed, has been broken. It's my guess that the key to making the ordinary seem extraordinary is never trying too hard. Opt for simplicity, stay classic and it's hard to go wrong. According to French model Inès de la Fressange, a desire to appear clever before appearing beautiful is what's really at the heart of style. And for me, that can never go out of fashion. — (M)

i

ABOUT THE WRITER: Sonia Zhuravlyova is a writer and sub editor at MONOCLE. She enjoys rummaging through rails of vintage clothes, trying to speak French and people watching on the streets of London and Paris.

ESSAY 06

Table talk

Plus ça change

A native's-eye view of any city is invaluable so pull up a chair at the nearest terrace table and eavesdrop on our very own café habitué as he shares his thoughts on a typical Paris morning.

by Raphaël Fejtö, author

I am sitting outside Le Progrès in the morning sun, reading *Libération* and enjoying a latte and a croissant.

Le Progrès is a timeless café in the heart of the Haut-Marais. The terrace, which juts out onto the intersection of Bretagne and Vieille du Temple like the prow of a ship, is furnished with simple wooden tables and chairs. The waiters here won't pretend to be your friend but nor will they spend time discussing their acting aspirations.

A beautiful girl is sitting at the table next to mine. She's focusing on her writing. She glances at me for a split second before returning to her thoughts. At another nearby perch sits Alain, a handsome man of about 75. Alain and I often cross paths in the morning and stop to chat. He used to work at *Lui* magazine, one of those grand French establishments of the 1970s. He went on to become an excellent cartoonist, funny and provocative, before dedicating himself to a career as a children's author.

I ask him why he stopped drawing. "I thought I could change the world," he says. "It turned out I couldn't so I stopped."

"Maybe you have changed it more than you think," I say.

I spot Matthew, an Asian-American writer. He likes to dress in head-to-toe black and always looks like he's moving in slow motion. He's written a tribute to *Faust*: a 1,500-page book in verse that none of us read. But we respect him for writing it. He says hello and heads off toward the *tabac*. Matthew smokes a lot. I think it's one of the reasons he's still in France.

Léa walks by in a hurry and gives me a quick smile. She works in Taeko, a Japanese canteen in the Enfant Rouge market that does the best bento in Paris. When I first met Léa she used to flirt with me but by

Spots to overhear conversations

01 La Perle
To understand why French lovers are French lovers.

02 Le Jardin des Roses
To hear people talk about love.

03 Le Musée Picasso
To hear Parisians complain that it took so long to reopen this magical place.

> *"Along comes Charlotte on her bike, a woman who's elegant even in sweat pants... We talk about love"*

the time I got my act together to flirt back it was too late; she had found the love of her life. Three bearded hepcats wander in discussing the finer points of cucumber water. I ponder why we never see them with beards half grown: they just appear in full bloom. Do they hide away until they reach the stipulated length?

Along comes Charlotte on her bike, a woman who's elegant even in sweat pants. "I just ran eight kilometres," she says.

Charlotte and I talk about love. She is dating an actor-author. "I told him I would buy him a shirt from Charvet for his birthday but he's not called me back," she says. "Is that normal?" When Charlotte leaves, the beautiful girl at the next table turns to me. "Excuse me," she says with a charming British accent. "Do you know the way to the Picasso museum?"

I am sitting outside Le Progrès, with my *Libération,* a latte and a croissant. The world turns but, fortunately, some things never change. — (M)

ABOUT THE WRITER: Raphaël Fejtö, born in 1974, is the author of *La vie à deux, ou presque*. When he isn't writing, he makes films and illustrates children's book published by l'Ecole des Loisirs and Seuil. He lives in Paris.

ESSAY 07

Neighbourhood watch
The districts of Paris

Most Parisians will be happy to tell you which arrondissement is the worst and which is the best (clue: it's the one they live in) but don't be taken in by their snobbery. Every district has something particular to offer – provided it's not the 16th...

by Tom Burges Watson, Monocle

Visitors to Paris can feel puzzled by the system of arrondissements – the 20 administrative areas – into which the city is divided but the essence of the plan is simple. There are 14 neighbourhoods on the *Rive Droite* and six on the Left Bank, neatly encircled by the Périphérique ring road. This arrangement radiates outwards, clockwise from the 1st arrondissement, with Place de la Concorde and the Louvre as its centre.

This system dates back more than two centuries and has earned the French capital its reputation for being a collection of villages with their own peculiarities. Parisians like to find out early on in a conversation which arrondissement you live in, and you can tell from their resulting facial expressions that they have pigeonholed you. Traditionally 10 of the 20 districts vote for a local mayor from the political right, whereas the other 10 lean to the left. However, the character of each area is so distinct that not only political persuasion but also income brackets and professions can be accurately guessed from the final two digits of the Parisian postal code.

The monarchy and aristocracy may as well have kept their heads because snobbery is alive and well in Paris. There is a certain type of Parisian who boasts about never frequenting an arrondissement with two digits but rising property prices are forcing a change of heart.

One of the positive outcomes of that has been the makeover given to almost every arrondissement. No longer is any district a no-go area, although that can still be said of numerous suburbs. Even areas that were once deemed dangerous places at night, such as Belleville and Ménilmontant, are now considered the ultimate *branché* (fashionable) neighbourhoods.

As well as being the most central, the 1st and 2nd arrondissements are the least inhabited. The 2nd is particularly vibrant in the evenings and the medieval street, Rue Montorgueil, is a mainstay of the Parisian bar and café scene. Once a bustling hub for prostitution, the 2nd has taken on a new, vastly improved identity; some argue that it is now one of the most desirable areas of Paris.

All change?

01 11th arrondissement
The multicultural vibe lives on.

02 19th arrondissement
This formerly working-class district has had a spruce-up.

03 20th arrondissement
The birthplace of Édith Piaf, this district will almost certainly be the next bohemian boomtown.

"The monarchy may as well have kept their heads because snobbery is alive and well in Paris"

The ever-fashionable Marais district (which straddles the 3rd and 4th) has become as expensive as the 6th and 7th arrondissements, both in terms of property and eating out. Many independent boutiques have been forced to relocate and make way for international chains, which have done little for the area's charm. However, Marais' enduring appeal is its architecture: this is one of the few parts of Paris where 19th-century architect Baron Haussmann was least active and so the buildings, which in some cases date back to the 14th century, have been left untouched.

One Paris arrondissement abounding in stereotypes is the 16th. Those who live in this largely residential district consider it the pinnacle of elegance and there is an inexplicable pride associated with having the 75016 postcode; that's Parisian snobbery in full flow. However, for the residents of the other 19 arrondissements "*le seizième*" is utterly boring, with little of interest to see or do in the area.

Many Parisians remain very attached to their individual quartier. Whether it is the familiar style of architecture, the nearby *tabacs*, the local brasserie or the weekly market, there are magnetic elements that make staying within the confines of your own district infinitely preferable. Venturing beyond one's own arrondissement can feel like a mission into unknown, hostile territory. — (M)

i

ABOUT THE WRITER: Born in Belgium, raised in Italy, the UK and Japan, Tom Burges Watson has been living in Paris since 2008. As well as being MONOCLE's Paris correspondent, he also hosts the evening news on France 24.

ESSAY 08

Tango 3.0
Musical Paris

One of the founders of Gotan Project, which has breathed new life into tango, traces the multi-ethnic influences of Paris and its pulsating nightclubs that run through his music.

by Philippe Cohen Solal, musician

Before I guide you through my Paris and introduce you to its music venues, I'd like to say a little about our culture. It is not an unfounded cliché to say that we kiss on the street (a lot), drink wine (a lot) and like to smoke on café terraces in a *pas mal* (not bad) quantity too.

Pas mal. It's a very Parisian expression. It is what we use when we are happy or like something. When we agree, we say *grave* ("sure") and when we're enthusiastic, it's *mortel* ("sick") or *carrément mortel* ("really sick"). But when we dislike something, it gets an indifferent *limite* ("so-so").

Our lingo has a special place in our hearts but what about our lungs? Well, they're clogged with smoke, as much from city traffic as those cigarettes. But before lighting up, any night out in Paris must begin with dinner. This is the great gulf that separates the French from English: it is inconceivable that a Frenchman would go out on the town without sitting down for dinner first. You must eat well if you are to drink well; fortunately it's easy to do both in the bistros near the Canal Saint-Martin, such as my favourite Le Verre Volé (*see page 31*).

Cohen Solal's iconic Parisian musicians

01 Thomas Bangalter "Half of Daft Punk, he's smart and humble."
02 Camille "She uses her voice and body as musical instruments."
03 Benjamin Biolay "He collects sensitive songs and beautiful women."

The golden triangle of Parisian nightlife is between the Canal Saint-Martin, Place de la République and Strasbourg Saint-Denis; and Montparnasse, Saint-Germain-des-Prés, Saint-Michel and the Left Bank are a little dead. Of course they're beautiful and so *pas mal* but quite frankly they're have-beens. And as we say in France, one cannot both be and have been – *on ne peut pas être et avoir été.*

Now let's visit the place that made me who I am. You'll have to forgive me if I fall into Parisian slang from time to time. My arrondissement, the 10th, is equivalent to London's Brixton. The north and the east of Paris are the home of music and food. You'll find African barbers, Kurdish kebab houses, Mauritian grocers, Indian, Pakistani and Bengali restaurants all rubbing along together to a multi-ethnic soundtrack that runs through my own music.

I write these lines the day after the 13 November terror attacks in Paris, which touched hearts across the capital and shook its artistic soul. Neo-bistros, hipster bars and our good old Bataclan: that infamously cramped yet vibrant concert hall. I know it well. My band Gotan Project [a Latin-and-tango infused electro group] played our first gig there back in

February 2002. The queue stretched the length of two streets and the hall was so packed that people in the audience swooned from the heat.

Carlos Gardel, the pioneer of tango, had much the same effect on his audience with his velvety voice a century before. In the same era, singer Maurice Chevalier – as recognisable in his straw hat as Daft Punk in their helmets today – tasted his first real success at the same venue. Decades later The Velvet Underground made their Paris debut at the club in 1972. It's difficult to express how dear the Bataclan is to Paris.

"Paris has always been the second home of tango. Born in the suburbs of Buenos Aires, the early adopters of this music were the porteños (port residents)"

I live a mere 20 metres from New Morning, the temple of jazz and world music that nonetheless regularly attracts baby rockers looking to compete in Emergenza – the festival for unsigned bands. This place is consistently *pas mal* but when Prince arrives there for his after-shows it's *mortel.*

Further along Rue des Petites Ecuries you'll find Studio Bleu, where my band rehearse before we go on tour. This space thuds with blasts of Brazilian *batucada*, reggae and old-school tango day and night. Here you'll find dancers preparing for the capital's tango balls, known by their Spanish name *milongas.*

I discovered tango and the Argentine composer Astor Piazzolla at 19 while nosing about in the record collection belonging to my then-girlfriend Prisca Lobjoy's parents. But then, Paris has always been the second home of tango. Born in the suburbs of Buenos Aires, the early adopters of this music were the bad boy *porteños* (port residents). It was accepted by the Argentine bourgeoisie only after it became popular with the elite in Paris in the early 20th century. In 1954, Piazzolla travelled to Paris to study with Nadia Boulanger, a friend of Stravinsky and a composition professor who went on to teach the likes of Aaron Copland, Philip Glass and Quincy Jones. It was under her impetus that Piazzolla created what would become Nuevo Tango and revolutionise the genre, taking it from the underground dance floors to prestigious ballrooms, just as Gershwin did with jazz.

In the 1970s many Argentinians fled to Paris to escape the military dictatorship and the club Trottoirs de Buenos Aires, an old grocery warehouse in Les Halles, became an epicentre for Argentine culture in the city. This was where art figures such as musical group Sexteto Mayor, *bandoneon* player Juan José Mosalini, musician Gustavo Beytelmann and writer Julio Cortázar crossed paths in the 1980s. Mosalini's son Juan Jo became our *bandoneon* player on tour and Beytelman has played piano and arranged strings on all our albums. He became our George Martin (if only we were The Beatles).

For an authentic glimpse of tango today, I recommend Contradanza XXL, a monthly tango ball held in the loft of the Bellevilloise arts centre at the heart of the Ménilmontant quarter. Founded in 1877 near Père Lachaise cemetery, right after the Commune, La Bellevilloise was the first Parisian co-operative built to offer to the middle classes access to political education and culture. Nowadays, its old, beautiful parquet floors and the DJs and musicians – often directly from Buenos Aires – create an atmosphere where past and present, north and south, merge for a *carrément mortel* authentic experience. — (M)

i

ABOUT THE WRITER: Philippe Cohen Solal is a French producer, composer, DJ, and co-founder of the multi-award-winning band Gotan Project. When he's not busy creating music for his record label ¡Ya Basta! Records or travelling the world performing, he can be found in the "golden triangle" enjoying a gig.

ESSAY 09

Modern masters

Future perfect

It's not all about picture-perfect cobbled streets and romantic vistas. Whether you love them or loathe them, visitors should make time for Paris's stark experiments with modernism.

by David Plaisant, Monocle

About 10 years ago I found myself changing lines on the Paris Metro. A usually banal experience, you may think, but that was before I encountered the *trottoir roulant rapide* (rapid moving walkway) or the TRR at the Montparnasse-Bienvenüe interchange. As I approached a long tunnel that stretched several hundred metres into the distance, a looped Tannoy rather aggressively warned "*Attention les pieds! Attention les pieds! Attention les pieds*!" This was accompanied by a flashing screen that warned that elderly, infant and infirm commuters should not board the TRR. Somewhat alarmed, I succumbed to this piece of pedestrian infrastructure.

A walkway like no other, it moved at some 9km per hour. It first transported users on to a slow-moving section, rollers then sped up to reach cruising speed, which really was rather *rapide*. The roller pads decelerated at the end of the tunnel but not before the robotic bleating of "*Attention les pieds!*" could be heard once more. This is for the space-age flâneur, a metropolitan epiphany of speed, I thought to myself and instantly got on the TRR again.

And Paris, despite its quaint quartiers, belle époque beauty and art nouveau indulgence can also be a city of modernity. In 1967 *Paris Match* published a special issue entitled *Paris dans 20 ans*; the cover, featuring the gleaming towers of steel and glass of the yet-to-be-built La Défense, is a remarkably accurate depiction of what stands today on the city's western edge. As the magazine details, however, this was only one of 50 sectors that were to be built; the city would be dotted with concrete megastructures and monumental brutalist edifices.

Modernist wonders

01 **Les Orgues de Flandre**
1970s modernism with diagonal tower blocks.

02 **Pont de Grenelle**
See the replica of the Statue of Liberty and the Front de Seine.

03 **Maison de la Radio France**
Franco-Orwellian architecture on a huge scale.

This was the brave new era of architecture where the vision of Le Corbusier was still pertinent. "The street is no more than a trench, a deep cleft, a narrow passage," he proclaimed in his 1925 *Plan Voisin* for Paris. As you cross the Seine from the 16th to the 15th arrondissements, a menacing vision of Corbusian Paris appears before you: the Front de Seine (or Beaugrenelle) district with 20 or so towers set on an elevated decking. Here, as Le Corb instructed, the street has been eradicated and in its place gardens and plazas are interspersed with buildings named Tour Cristal, Tour Évasion 2000, Tour Mars and even a cosmically named community centre: "Mercure III".

The postwar Parisian space odyssey can be an unsettling experience and doesn't come without its detractors. Directly above that futuristic *trottoir rapide* stands the monolithic Tour Montparnasse that, after completion in 1973, has undoubtedly become Paris's most loathed building. The year the tower was completed was also the year that gave Paris another infamous construction: the Boulevard Périphérique, the six-lane motorway that determines the administrative boundaries of Paris. The 35km road that orbits the Département 75 is now the busiest in Europe and it's hard to romanticise its congested underpasses, greying walls and seedy slip roads. It does, however, much like the Tour Montparnasse, provide the visitor with a rude awakening: Paris is no theatre set. It is real and abruptly modern.

"Paris, despite its quaint quartiers, belle époque beauty and art nouveau indulgence can also be a city of modernity"

Recently I descended below the hated tower at Montparnasse with the express purpose of boarding that speedy marvel of a walkway. The tunnel was there but where were the flashing screens? I couldn't hear the robotic tones telling me to watch my feet. Here was nothing but a standard, if very long, moving walkway, with one speed and no frightening warnings. Bereft, I asked a guard what had happened to the *trottoir roulant rapide* only to hear the apologetic reply: "Monsieur, we had to rip it out years ago."

Perhaps unsurprisingly, the walkway resulted in too many injuries due to the complex nature of boarding and dismounting. The TRR, like much of postwar Paris, was that bit too modern for Parisians and visitors alike. Modern Paris can be scary and it can be a little too *rapide* sometimes; just enough, you could say, to keep you on your toes. — (M)

i

ABOUT THE WRITER: David Plaisant was MONOCLE's design correspondent. He now lives and works in Rome, where he continues to write for us.

ESSAY 10

Immovable feasts
Food culture

If you want to eat at a particular Parisian restaurant, don't do so on a whim: opening times – and days – are scrupulously observed. Here's why embracing the fussiness will heighten your dining experience.

by Sarah Moroz, journalist

3 favourite French food norms

01 Grabbing a still-warm pain au chocolat in the morning.
02 Tossing back oysters at the *marché*.
03 That indispensable breadbasket at every meal.

The connection between France and the delights of the palate is inextricable. Paris especially is a place of quotidian hedonism, small-scale but high intensity. It's the impulsiveness of ripping into a baguette before you've even left the boulangerie, or the offhand attitude to drinking wine in your lunch hour. Even the culinary terminology is a lavish subset within the language: vol-au-vent; mousseline; bisque; sabayon; rémoulade; langoustine. Each word unspools technique and tradition with a uniquely bewitching sound.

For a newcomer, the ritual around the French meal itself can be startling. The requisite components that make up the framework for eating – entrée, *plat*, dessert – were not a regimen I had ever followed assiduously. Hailing from North America, I was used to different portions and indiscriminate meal times; in fact, I was rather partial to my native snack-happy culture. I would be nourished hither and thither, sometimes completely arbitrarily with a mid-afternoon granola bar or a post-midnight slice of pizza.

In France a meal is always accompanied by good fresh bread and concluded with an espresso, and restaurants are open only at certain hours and on certain days. I adapted grudgingly at first but, as time passed, my attitude to consumption began to change. The effect was to make me think of mealtime as a sliver of the day that warranted careful consideration; this is not a culture in which you absentmindedly eat lunch at your desk, nor dinner in front of the television. Meals are a serious business, feeding discussion and perpetuating tradition; a kind of daily sacrament.

The city's markets also changed my approach to eating. The *marché* is the quintessentially popular (as in "of the people") spot for buying quality produce, where you know you are buying seasonal food because that is all traders offer. Market stands cite the provenance of their produce on little chalkboards suspended from their stalls, which are also a clue to what's fresh in restaurants, as any good menu will change depending on what the *marché* has to offer. The inclination to eat seasonally is pervasive and the consequent changes to dishes mean there are always surprises.

The French idea of cuisine has progressed away from stodgy classics and is now often driven by chefs from elsewhere or natives who have worked abroad and returned with fresh ideas. However, cultural remixes doesn't always yield French-flavoured finesse: sometimes you just end up with a pointless pastiche of other cultures. There's also a lament that valued French traditions are being eroded by the worst of fast-food culture, whether in the form of a refrigerated sandwich at Monoprix or the queues at McDonald's.

"Within days of the November 2015 terrorist attacks, citizens were urged to flock to restaurants, bistros, bars and cafés"

Other elements around dining remain controversial. A debate broke out a few years ago about whether the label *Fait maison* (Homemade) should be present on restaurant menus. It was said that such a label, with an identifiable logo, would allow diners to identify which restaurants prepare fresh dishes on site using raw, unprocessed ingredients. This was seen as a countermeasure to the industrially bought foods that middling brasseries and their ilk reheat and serve. The procedures for implementing these measures remain unresolved, complicated by the fact that some restaurants prepare dishes fresh on site but use certain pre-bought products.

Taking time to eat together, however, remains a defining aspect of Parisian identity. Within days of the November 2015 terrorist attacks, restaurant authority Le Guide Fooding started a campaign called *Tous au Bistrot* (Everyone to the Bistro). The initiative urged citizens to flock to restaurants, bistros, bars and cafés in defiance of the fear momentarily sown into urban living. Basking in bold flavours as an act of resistance couldn't be more French; a nation determined to eat well – and live well – in good times and bad. — (M)

i

ABOUT THE WRITER: Born and raised in New York, Sarah Moroz moved to Paris in 2009. She is a freelance journalist, working for various publications including MONOCLE, and is a fan of the cheese course.

ESSAY 11

Parisian pluck
Shaping the world

Are the French justified in feeling extremely pleased with themselves about their achievements in the fields of industry, culture and the arts? *Mais oui*, says our writer, and with very good reason.

by Amy Richardson, writer

In 2013, a survey by Washington-based Pew Research Centre confirmed the truth of an oft-repeated stereotype: that the French are considered to be some of the most arrogant people in Europe. (The surprise? Even the French agreed.) But the question is this: isn't arrogance justified – and acceptable – if your country is just better than almost every other, at almost everything?

Pick any industry or creative field, be it art, fashion, food, film, literature, philosophy, urban planning or architecture, and there's a Frenchman (or Frenchwoman) who has kicked down the door and not given two flying baguettes as to what people thought of them in the process – even the word "entrepreneur" is French.

At the Dôme des Invalides in the 7th arrondissement lies the tomb of Napoleon, a man who had more success in bending the world to his will – and perhaps more accusations of arrogance flung his way – than any other in history.

His subjects – who at the turn of the 19th century meant countries from Portugal to Egypt – received directives about all aspects of their life: civil servants were instructed to bring more suitable girlfriends to public outings, parish priests were reprimanded for poor pulpit performances, while each night, the long-suffering Empress Joséphine had her clothing picked out for her for the following day (something that must have driven the infamous clothes horse up the chinoiserie-papered palace wall). No aspect of public and private life was too mundane for Napoleon's in-depth musings and his merciless reforms. But did he care what the recipients of his micro-managing missives thought of him? *Mon dieu, non.*

France has also impacted the world in ways that are more tangible to the casual visitor. Pick up any fashion magazine (incidentally, another Gallic invention) and the first 20 pages or so will most likely read as a roll call of French designers – Chanel, Saint Laurent, Celine, Dior – a list mirrored by a wander down Avenue Champs-Élysées and its fashion houses. Today the country's luxury-goods market (champagne, fashion, leather goods) contributes a whopping €217bn to the global economy. The French have been dictating what the world has worn since the 17th century when fashionable types all over Europe lost their heads for the exquisitely crafted baroque and then rococo fashions modelled by the Bourbon monarchs in the court of Versailles (a trend personified by the tragic figure of Marie Antoinette, who had hers lopped off by the revolutionaries in 1793 thanks to her excessive love of French fripperies).

3 historic sites

01 Vendôme Column, Place Vendôme
This bas relief portrays scenes of Napoleon's triumph at Austerlitz.

02 Place de la Concorde
Where Marie-Antionette and many others met the guillotine.

03 Chanel, 31 Rue Chambon
Coco Chanel opened this shop in 1921.

"It's not simply ability and skill that distinguishes the Parisian creative; it's vision and chutzpah"

Unlike Britain, France didn't go through a rapid period of industrialisation at the turn of the 19th century so its skilled artisans were able to continue turning out their laborious, finely crafted furniture, porcelain, leather goods and textiles in peace. This is just one of the reasons Paris continues to be the world's premier shopping destination.

But it's not simply ability and skill that distinguishes the Parisian creative; it's vision backed up by a whole lot of chutzpah. When Coco Chanel decided to don a pair of men's trousers to better ride her horse, she single-handedly revolutionised the way women wore clothes (although she later bemoaned the trend: "Having 70 per cent of women wearing trousers at evening dinner is quite sad"). She went on to change the perfume industry, pioneered the use of comfortable fabrics such as jersey and cotton and made the little black dress iconic. "I don't care what you think about me," she famously said to her detractors. "I don't think about you at all."

In 2010 Unesco tapped another French industry for "intangible world heritage" – its cuisine. While French trends have been prescribing global food trends since the Middle Ages, in the 20th century chef and restaurateur Georges

Auguste Escoffier simplified and codified French cookery techniques and forever changed the way we think about food. (Some of his other achievements include the invention of the à la carte menu and commercially canned tomatoes.) The cookery school bearing his name at the Ritz Hotel continues to instruct new generations of chefs and also offers casual classes for visitors.

Other notable historic sites and figures are covered at length by other essays in this guide. Le Corbusier, that most beloved and maligned of all architects, left his modernist fingerprints on almost every major city in the world (*see page 118*). Paris was the birthplace of modern cinema (*see Eugenia Ellanskaya's essay on page 72*), the literary epicentre of the world in the 20th century (*see Marie-Sophie Schwarzer's essay on this page*) and gave rise to the major art movements of the 19th and 20th centuries (impressionism, symbolism, cubism and art deco, to name but a few).

The French just have that certain *je ne sais quoi* and vision that allows them to shape the world – and influence the rest of us in the process. So who can blame them for feeling a little superior? — (M)

i

ABOUT THE WRITER: Writer Amy Richardson edited this guide. She enjoys strolling the streets of Paris and wondering about the historic icons who have done the same.

ESSAY 12

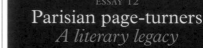

Parisian page-turners
A literary legacy

You don't have to go far to find an independent bookshop in a city that's steeped in the history of Balzac, Zola and Hemingway. So let's begin at the beginning – with Shakespeare and Company.

by Marie-Sophie Schwarzer, Monocle

"There's so much nostalgia. It's not the same city that Hemingway came to in the 1920s – but it's Paris," says Sylvia Beach Whitman, owner of the city's Anglophone islet of literature: the Notre Dame-facing bookshop Shakespeare and Company.

Opened by her father George Whitman in 1951, it's inspired by Sylvia Beach's original Shakespeare and Company at 12 Rue de l'Odéon, which published James Joyce's *Ulysses* in 1922 and was a haven for the likes of Gertrude Stein, Ezra Pound and TS Eliot. The City of Lights – and this bookshop in its various incarnations – has been home to the Lost Generation, the Beat

Generation and today a new generation of writers seeking inspiration in the labyrinthine cobbled streets of Paris. If it's not clear immediately, it certainly becomes apparent as soon as you step inside the book-lined space: the French capital is a magnet for readers and writers alike.

The city has long been the cultural beacon of Europe but it was at the zenith of *les années folles* in the 1920s – an era so dazzlingly recalled in Ernest Hemingway's memoir *A Moveable Feast* – that Paris established itself as the world's literary capital. Sure, Voltaire made waves in the 18th century and novelists Honoré de Balzac, George Sand and Émile Zola left their marks, but the cosmopolitan charm and promise that Paris projects to this day stems from a time when international writers and artists such as Pablo Picasso and Hemingway sat side by side and made the most extraordinary art by drawing on the French way of life. It's the period that inspired Woody Allen's film *Midnight in Paris*, scenes from which inevitably play in your mind's eye as you stroll down Rue Bonaparte past the Abbey of Saint-Germain-des-Prés, ideally nibbling on a *fleur de sel* caramel macaron.

"If you are lucky enough to have lived in Paris as a young man, then wherever you go for the rest of your life it stays with you, for Paris is a moveable feast," wrote Hemingway in 1950. The US author was a leading figure of the Lost Generation that flocked to Paris in the 1920s, disillusioned and alienated by the First World War and yearning for the bohemian liberty that the French capital promised. He spent close to a decade roaming the Left Bank and wrote some of his most prominent novels during his stay, including *The Sun Also Rises* and *Men Without Women.* Along the way he met Fitzgerald and Joyce and spent many hours at the original Shakespeare and Company. And while it's easy to get lost in a haze of nostalgia – much has changed since those days – it's impossible not to be moved by the city's poetry: the serpentine Seine, the sparkling Eiffel Tower and the sidewalk cafés that offer front-row seats to the bustling theatre of street life. Hemingway and Joyce were loyal patrons at Les Deux Magots and Café de Flore in Saint-Germain-des-Prés for that very reason.

> *"Ernest Hemingway and James Joyce were loyal patrons at Les Deux Magots and Café de Flore in Saint-Germain-des-Prés"*

While such historic institutions are now crowded with tourists, anyone strolling through Paris will quickly discover that the culture of reading is still strong here. When you board a bus or train in New York or London you'll encounter people whose eyes are glued to glowing screens or a tattered copy of the *Metro* newspaper but in Paris they'll more likely be clutching a yellow-leafed edition of Albert Camus's existential tale *The Stranger*. Walking along the banks of the Seine you'll witness a cross-section of Parisians sharing bottles of wine and flicking through Marcel Proust's *In Search of Lost Time*.

Paris's affiliation with literature was reaffirmed more than half a century after Hemingway's *A Moveable Feast* was published, when Parisians left copies of the book among tributes to the victims of the November 2015 terrorist attacks. It was a defiant, symbolic celebration of the city; a gesture to show that in the face of so much death, Paris was still about living. This keen sense of vivaciousness is also true of the city's bookshops. Whereas across the Channel in the UK more than 500 independent booksellers have closed their doors since 2005, Sylvia's Shakespeare and Company is one of thousands thriving in Paris.

Among them is the city's oldest bookshop Librairie Delamain, dating from the 1700s, as well as the 200 or so *bouquinistes* perched along the Seine. France regularly invests millions in the industry, well aware that book sales make up about 50 per cent of its cultural produce nationwide. It's no surprise that the nation is home to more winners of the Nobel prize for literature than any other country.

Whatever the future holds and however many bookshops grace its winding streets in years to come, Paris will always be the city of Hemingway and Fitzgerald, of Voltaire and Picasso, and a refuge for readers, writers and flâneurs eager to soak up the sights and sounds – not least of the nearest independent bookshop. New York may be the star on the silver screen and London may provide the world's soundtrack but Paris inspires the words. "Seeing the city through the window of my bookshop is magical," says Beach Whitman. "Every once in a while someone will come in and say, 'Are you Sylvia? I'm the new James Joyce. It's nice to meet you.'" — (M)

City classics

01 Victor Hugo's **Notre Dame de Paris** (*The Hunchback of Notre Dame*), 1831
02 Émile Zola's **Au Bonheur des Dames** (*The Ladies' Delight*), 1883
03 Gertrude Stein's ***Paris France***, 1940
04 Jack Kerouac's **Satori in Paris**, 1966

i

ABOUT THE WRITER: Marie-Sophie Schwarzer is an associate editor at MONOCLE. She was delighted to return to Paris for the purpose of this guide, having spent a spring term there once upon a time studying French at the Sorbonne – and making daily visits to Shakespeare and Company. No wonder she's so well read.

Culture
— Sights and sounds

Some disparage Paris as a staid and stuffy "city of museums". It's true that it has more cultural institutions than any other – 468 cinemas, museums, opera houses and theatres at last count – so picking your way through can be a challenge. But this section will steer you in the right direction (and hopefully away from the camera-toting hordes). Here we've given preference to cultural gems that narrow their focus, whether on the lifework of a solo artist or a quirky sub-genre such as antique fairground gadgets.

Paris has one of the most rambunctious art scenes in the world. Mixed-use hubs such as La Gaîté Lyrique and Le Bal prove that the city's creatives are looking to the future and its commercial galleries represent some of the most exploratory and cutting-edge artists in the world.

This section also lists our favourite cinemas and, if you're looking for something a little more upbeat, our pick of the music venues. But for perhaps the most authentic experience of all, head to a riverside *guinguette* (dance hall) with Parisians of all ages and shimmy the night away to some traditional tunes.

Galleries and museums
Paint the town

① Musée des Arts Forains, Bercy (12e)
Fair play

Evoke your inner child at this whimsical museum dedicated to fairgrounds and their associated paraphernalia dating from 1850 to 1950. This magical and lovingly restored world is the private collection of antiques dealer and actor Jean Paul Favand, which he opens up to the public by appointment.

Ride a colourful wooden carousel, watch an Italian opera performed by mechanical puppets and be transformed into otherworldly shapes by magic mirrors in pavilions. This place has to be seen to be believed.

53 Avenue des Terroirs de France, 75012
+33 (0)1 4340 1622
arts-forains.com

② Palais Galliera, Trocadéro (16e)
Model museum

This shrine to fashion presents temporary exhibitions dedicated to the clothing industry and its creators. The spotlight is often on French designers and the museum also draws on its Musée Carnavalet collection of historic garments, costumes, accessories and photography.

The Palais Galliera reopened in 2013 after a major overhaul: the walls were returned to their original Pompeiian-red colour scheme and a new lighting system was installed. Bear in mind that it's closed when there isn't an exhibition; on Thursdays it's open until 21.00.

10 Rue Pierre 1er de Serbie, 75116
+33 (0)1 5652 8600
palaisgalliera.paris.fr

I got a little carried away at Musée des Arts Forains

3

Musée Nissim de Camondo, Monceau (8e)
Family matters

Count Moïse de Camondo, a French banker and art collector of Ottoman origin, built this sumptuous neoclassical house in 1911: it's modelled on the Petit Trianon, a small château in Versailles. The interiors are replete with the count's art collections and the Orloff silver dinner set commissioned by Catherine II of Russia.

Moïse donated the house to Les Art Décoratifs when his son Nissim died in 1917. It became a museum in 1935 and is named, as the count wished, after his son.
63 Rue de Monceau, 75008
+33 (0)1 5389 0650
lesartsdecoratifs.fr

Art house

Rodin lived and worked in the Hôtel Biron

④

Musée Rodin, Invalides (7e)

Set in stone

The 18th-century Hôtel Biron recently underwent a three-year €16m renovation. Rodin's former home and studio has been a museum since 1919 and has unsurprisingly suffered significant wear and tear; the sculptor's heavier works took their toll. Today the structure has been refurbished from the cornices to the flooring and Rodin's works have been brought back out of storage.

Highlights of Rodin's extensive collection of Etruscan and Roman sculptures include his renowned "The Thinker" – displayed in the gardens – and the Greek-inspired "The Walking Man". Also on show are works by his pupil and lover Camille Claudel and rare masterpieces by Edvard Munch and Vincent van Gogh, Rodin's contemporaries. The refreshed *musée* sheds a new and fitting light on the sculptor.

77 Rue de Varenne, 75007
+33 (0)1 4418 6110
musee-rodin.fr

Near and deer
—
Antlers et al are prized by this hunting museum

⑤

Musée de la Chasse et de la Nature, Le Marais (3e)

Thrill of the chase

A word of warning: people who find taxidermy on the nose should stay well away from this museum. But those who don't mind seeing exotic animals displayed in bizarre ways will discover an extensive and fascinating collection of hunting trophies, vintage weapons and modern and antique artwork related to *la chasse*.

The private collection was founded in 1964 by hunting enthusiasts François and Jacqueline Sommer and is housed in two beautiful *hôtel particuliers*. Around one corner a group of baboons smoke cigars and play cards. Another room features an installation of owls by contemporary Belgian artist Jan Fabre; the birds observe visitors and create a macabre ceiling with their feathered bodies. The galleries of mother-of-pearl-inlaid hunting rifles are another highlight.

60 Rue des Archives, 75003
+33 (0)1 5301 9240
chassenature.org

⑥

Palais de Tokyo, Trocadéro (16e)

Bright future

Just a stroll from the Eiffel Tower, this building is a futuristic exhibition space for contemporary international art. Across four floors, experimental and thought-provoking shows create an interactive wonder factory.

In the eastern wing you'll find the Musée d'Art Moderne de la Ville de Paris, with a permanent collection including work by the likes of Picasso and Matisse. But there's always something new to discover here. Magazine aficionados will enjoy browsing the super selection of international titles in the shop.

13 Avenue du Président Wilson, 75116
+33 (0)1 8197 3588
palaisdetokyo.com

⑦

Musée Picasso Paris, Le Marais (3e)

Life of the artist

After a much-needed renovation, the Musée Picasso Paris reopened its doors to the public in 2014. In the refurbished 17th-century building sits a methodically plotted-out selection of works by the late great.

The collection reveals details of the artist's daily practices, captures his emergence into cubism and documents the figurative transformation of his wife Olga from object of affection into ugly obscurity. Other interesting exhibits include scribblings from his fleeting sojourn into poetry and an entire room dedicated to his oddball eroticism.

5 Rue de Thorigny, 75003
+33 (0)1 8556 0036
museepicassoparis.fr

⑧

Musée des Arts Décoratifs, Louvre (1er)

History lesson

This museum, which occupies part of the Louvre, is dedicated to decorative arts and furniture that range from the Renaissance to the present day. Don't miss the jewellery gallery, with more than 1,000 pieces glistening under spotlights, or the furniture section with works by the likes of Robert Mallet-Stevens.

The temporary-exhibition schedule covers everything from international fashion to wallpaper. And the gallery shop is one of the best, whether you're after books, magazines or designer homeware.

107 Rue de Rivoli, 75001
+33 (0)1 4455 5750
lesartsdecoratifs.fr

9

Petit Palais, Champs-Élysées (8e)
One for all

Built in 1900 in the beaux arts style, this museum was architect Charles Girault's ode to the creativity of the early 20th century. Its mural-decorated lobbies, galleries and ornate cupolas now house a permanent collection of art spanning from sculptures from ancient Greece to photography of the 19th century.

You'll find paintings and sculptures by Pissarro, Cézanne, Rodin and Delacroix overseen by a series of busts of Parisian art luminaries set into the walls. And unlike many of the city's other art institutions, you won't have to battle it out with crowds of tourists to get a look at them.

But it's the temporary exhibitions that really make this a must-visit. Recent displays have ranged from the fashion of Yves Saint Laurent to the macabre drawings and etchings of Goya and the wood-block prints of Japanese artist Kuniyoshi. There's also a lovely café in the mosaic-tiled courtyard where you can have a coffee once you're done perusing the collections.

Avenue Winston Churchill, 75008
+33 (0)1 5343 4000
petitpalais.paris.fr

Four more

01 **Muséum National d'Histoire Naturelle, Pantheon:** This antique research institution became a natural-history museum during the French Revolution and now hosts a four-storey taxidermy collection and thousands of geological and anatomical samples. Leave time for a stroll through the Jardin des Plantes, a medicinal herb garden designed for 17th-century monarch Louis XIII.
mnhn.fr

02 **Musée d'Orsay, Palais-Bourbon:** The Musée d'Orsay's barrel vault and giant clock incite flashbacks of its past life as a train station. Inaugurated as a museum in 1986, it fills the 1848 to 1914 gap left largely uncovered by the Louvre and Pompidou. Expect a broad gamut of impressionist and post-impressionist art.
musee-orsay.fr

03 **Musée de l'Orangerie, Louvre:** Unlike the Musée d'Orsay, this impressionist collection across the Seine is a solo project. The museum's airy halls were given the tick of approval by Claude Monet to house his "Water Lilies", which extend across 91 metres of canvas. A permanently mounted must-see.
musee-orangerie.fr

04 **Musée d'Art Moderne de la Ville de Paris, Champs-Élysées:** Free entry to Mam's permanent collections invites viewers to see 8,000 works from the 20th and 21st centuries. A highlight? Dufy's "The Electricity Fairy", a vast illuminated mural encapsulating the history and application of electricity.
mam.paris.fr

(10)

La Maison Rouge, Quai de la Rapée (12e)
Big shot

Photography enthusiast Antoine de Galbert founded this private foundation in 2003 to promote contemporary photography through a roster of temporary exhibitions. The gallery throws the spotlight on private collections and the people behind them, such as Artur Walther who spent 20 years accruing an assembly of German, US, African and Asian photography.

The building in the Bastille district was once a factory and still retains an industrial vibe in a space designed by Jean-Michel Alberola.
10 Boulevard de la Bastille, 75012
+33 (0)1 4001 0881
lamaisonrouge.org

(11)

Jeu de Paume, Tuileries (8e)
About time

Built at the edge of the Jardin des Tuileries, this often overlooked gallery presents photography, video, installations and web-art. From Florence Henri to Ai Weiwei, the gallery aspires to construct a dialogue between the likes of poetry and politics, past and present.
1 Place de la Concorde, 75008
+33 (0)1 4703 1250
jeudepaume.org

Commercial galleries
Off the wall

(1)

Thaddaeus Ropac, Le Marais (3e)
Change of place

"The art world has changed considerably in the past 30 years," says gallery owner Thaddaeus Ropac. "When I began it was a small ivory tower whereas today it has become tentacular." The Austrian-born curator's galleries have also followed this trend: he founded his first gallery in Salzburg, opened this Parisian space in 1990 and established another in Pantin in 2012.

Ropac's renown in the world of contemporary-art dealing – thanks to his oversight of artists such as Anslem Kiefer and Gilbert and George, as well as the foundation for late Italian painter Emilio Vedova – has gained him a loyal clientele of European collectors. A former printing space, his Le Marais gallery is flooded with natural light, creating a tranquil setting for the works of art.
7 Rue Debelleyme, 75003
+33 (0)1 4272 9900
ropac.net

2

Kamel Mennour, Saint-Germain-des-Prés (6e)
What's in a name?

Algerian-born, French-raised gallery owner Kamel Mennour opened his first space, south of the Seine, in 1999. He now has two locations in Saint-Germain-des-Prés and one in the 8th arrondissement. "After the Sixties, Paris lost her place in the art world but now we see that the city has again become seductive for artists, curators and collectors," he says.

With a sterling international reputation, Mennour has represented distinguished talent but it's not all about the big names: he's always on the lookout for unsigned talent.
47 Rue Saint-André Des Arts, 75006
+33 (0)1 5624 0363
kamelmennour.com

All sorts
—
Artists of all ages show at Almine Rech

3

VnH Gallery, Le Marais (3e)
New blood

Filling the shoes of previous gallery owner and avant-garde curator Yvon Lambert in 2015 was no small feat but Hélène Nguyen-Ban and Victoire de Pourtalès are rising to the challenge in their Le Marais space. "We respect Lambert's work but our aim is neither to follow his path nor to part with it," says De Pourtalès.

Beneath the glass-roofed interiors the duo have exhibited unusual works by artists from under-represented locations around the globe. A notable example was a show that explored voodooism by Cameroon-born artist Pascale Marthine Tayou.
108 Rue Vieille du Temple, 75003
+33 (0)1 8509 4321
vnhgallery.com

4

Almine Rech, Le Marais (3^{e})
Takes one to know one

Hidden behind looming white doors tagged with graffiti is Almine Rech's eponymous gallery, opened in 1997. An artist herself, Rech has long been a fixture of the Parisian art landscape.

Rech has established a robust stable of talent that includes the likes of Jeff Koons and Alex Israel. "It was always my idea to show artists without any generational prejudice," she says. Rech reminds collectors of artists who might otherwise fade into obscurity. "Art history isn't linear and sometimes we love, then we forget, then we love again."
64 Rue de Turenne, 75003
+33 (0)1 4583 7190
alminerech.com

5

Air de Paris, Chevaleret (13^{e})
Get the message

Founded in 1990 by Florence Bonnefous and Edouard Merino as a tribute to Marcel Duchamp and his work "Air de Paris", this gallery on the Left Bank resembles a residential building rather than an art space. That is, until you step inside.

The gallery boasts a portfolio of some 40 artists and what separates it from the pack is its desire to put across a message rather than display art for art's sake. "Our motifs are artistic, of course, but also intellectual and political," says curator Arlène Berceliot Courtin. "This identity has been in the making for 25 years."
32 Rue Louise Weiss, 75013
+33 (0)1 4423 0277
airdeparis.com

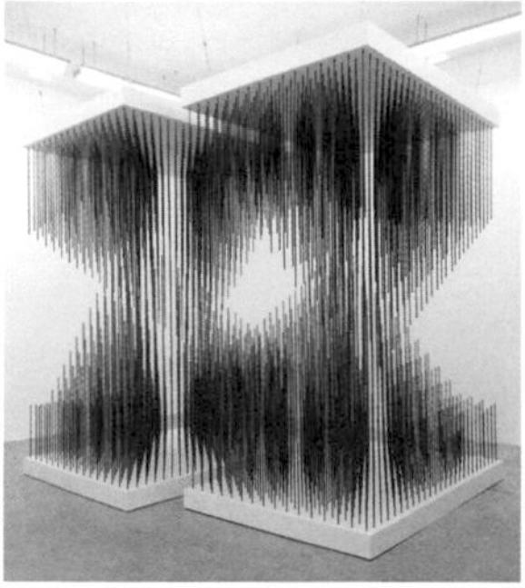

6
Galerie Perrotin, Le Marais (3^e)
Home is where the art is

Another of Le Marais' leading art haunts is Galerie Perrotin, which lies beyond a courtyard in a lofty two-storey converted residence. With two Paris locations and outposts in New York and Hong Kong, gallery owner Emmanuel Perrotin continues to act as a radical voice in the art world.
76 Rue de Turenne, 75003
+33 (0)1 4216 7979
perrotin.com

7
Marian Goodman, Le Marais (3^e)
Flexible fixture

Marian Goodman opened her gallery in Paris in 1995 and in the 17th-century Hôtel de Montmor she shows the work of some 40 artists. Six times a year the gallery changes shape to accommodate the photos, paintings and films created by both its A-list and up-and-coming cast.
79 Rue du Temple, 75003
+33 (0)1 4804 7052
mariangoodman.com

Other major sights

01 **Musée du Louvre, Louvre:** Minimise the stress of visiting one of the world's biggest and busiest museums by planning your route through its 35,000 artworks and antiquities. The throng of tourists also tends to calm post-lunch.
louvre.fr

02 **Eiffel Tower, Champ de Mars:** The "Iron Lady" was built in 1889 as a temporary installation but has become a permanent symbol of the city. You can ascend the 1,665 steps to the top but most people opt for the lift.
toureiffel.paris

03 **Arc de Triomphe, Champs-Élysées:** On the Place de l'Étoile, this 18th-century monument was built by Napoleon to pay tribute to his army. The "Unknown Soldier", a tomb dedicated to the fallen of the First World War, lies beneath and every day at 18.30 a flame of remembrance is lit.
arcdetriompheparis.com

04 **Jardin des Tuileries, Tuileries:** This archetypal Parisian garden between the Louvre and the Place de la Concorde is often full of tourists. Find a free bench in a quiet spot and enjoy views of the Seine or stroll around sculptures by Giacometti, Maillol and Rodin.
113 Rue de Rivoli, 75001

05 **Centre Pompidou, Beaubourg:** Behind this building's façade is one of Europe's most important collections of modern and contemporary art. As well as the exhibitions and the thousands of pieces on display from the permanent collection, the venue hosts screenings and live shows.
centrepompidou.fr

Cultural venues
Sites for sore eyes

1
La Gaîté Lyrique, Arts et Métiers (3e)
Get the picture

This multidisciplinary venue in the heart of Paris hosts exhibitions, lectures and film screenings, all of which revolve around web culture and digital art. The 19th-century building, which was formerly a theatre, has more than 9,500 sq m of space where visitors are invited to play video games, eat brunch, browse galleries dedicated to 3D animation and graphic design, take part in various coding workshops or even dance the night away at gigs; the musical roster ranges from electronic and house music to hip hop.

The venue also puts on regular presentations for those who work (or want to work) in the creative online industries, covering everything from recent innovations to entrepreneurism. This is a must-see for anyone interested in digital culture.
3 Bis Rue Papin, 75003
+33 (0)1 5301 5200
gaite-lyrique.net

②
Le Bal, Pigalle (18ᵉ)
Real deal

This cutting-edge exhibition space, near the bustling Avenue de Clichy, is a leading independent venue to catch some contemporary art. But to refer to Le Bal simply as a gallery would do the venue a disservice. It was once home to a risqué club and betting shop but in 2006 the City of Paris bought the decrepit building in the 18th arrondissement and transformed it into a cultural space with the help of the young architects at Agence Search.

Le Bal focuses on documentary and the different interpretations of "reality". It does this through an impressive education arm – Bal Lab – that holds talks, workshops and theatre performances, as well as exhibitions in the two gallery spaces. There is also an excellent bookshop and a café opens onto a communal garden where chic Parisians converge.
6 Impasse de la Défense, 75018
+33 (0)1 4470 7550
le-bal.fr

Music venues
Hear this

❶
L'Olympia, Madeleine (9ᵉ)
Centre stage

Of the countless music venues scattered around Paris, L'Olympia in the 9th arrondissement has played host to some of the biggest names in the business – and with good reason. Its size – 2,000 seats on the main floor, mezzanine and balcony – makes for the perfect venue to see an acclaimed act in an intimate setting.

Bruno Coquatrix's concert hall has put on almost every musician to have broken into the charts over the past century, including Édith Piaf, Ray Charles and the Arctic Monkeys. The unmistakable red neon sign emblazoned across the otherwise traditional Parisian townhouse is a reminder that this old city can still put on a fantastic show.
28 Boulevard des Capucines, 75009
+33 (0)1 892 683 368
olympiahall.com

②
Le Caveau de la Huchette, Latin Quarter (5ᵉ)
All that jazz

One of the city's best jazz clubs can be found in a wine cellar along the Rive Gauche. Grab a drink at the ground-floor bar before heading down to the basement, where you'll find a dance floor and stage with acts playing jazz, swing, soul and blues.
5 Rue de la Huchette, 75005
+33 (0)1 4326 6505
caveaudelahuchette.fr

New life

The Le 104 space, housed in a former funeral parlour, has become a cultural highlight in the still slightly gritty 19th arrondissement. It's now a base for resident artists and music organisations and the public can visit for film screenings, dance classes, music and exhibitions.
104.fr

③

Guinguette Chez Gégène, Joinville-le-Pont (outside 12e)
Let's dance

One of the most authentic places in Paris to soak up a little culture from yesteryear. A *guinguette* is a type of tavern-cum-dance-hall that originated in Belleville and Montmartre in the 18th century and then spread to areas along the Seine and Marne rivers. Chez Gégène on the outskirts of Paris is one of the last and it's well worth the travel time.

You'll feel projected into the past as you listen to traditional music and watch Parisians dance up a storm. Conventional French meals are served on red-and-white checked tables but the real attraction is the entertainment. It's not a good idea to take photos: many people are here with lovers rather than spouses, while others take dancing too seriously to let it be interrupted by a pic-snapping tourist. Bear in mind this venue is closed during low season.
162 Bis Quai de Polangis, 94340
+33 (0)1 4883 2943
chez-gegene.fr

④

La Cigale, Pigalle (18^{e})
Listen in

This staple of Parisian culture in the heart of Pigalle has provided the city with entertainment for more than a century. Despite its tumultuous history – including a brief spell as a kung fu cinema in the 1940s – the red-velvet-bedecked venue was brought back to life thanks to a redesign by French designer Philippe Starck in 1988.

La Cigale has since played host to some of the most exciting Parisian bands and DJs, as well as a good dose of internationally renowned entertainers: the likes of Prince and David Bowie have pranced across its stage. Today the musical offering tends towards the indie; a typical night out might involve a moody showing from Jamie XX or a rollicking set by Mac Demarco.
120 Boulevard de Rochechouart, 75018
+33 (0)1 4925 8999
lacigale.fr

Cinemas
Points to view

①

Louxor, Gare du Nord (10^{e})
Old school

A historic venue in Paris's 10th arrondissement, Louxor was reopened in 2013 after more than 30 years lying derelict. The quirky art deco-meets-ancient-Egyptian-themed decor has been faithfully restored to its 1920s splendour thanks to community action.

Today the three screening rooms, including a main theatre that seats more than 300 viewers, show a wide range of films, from mainstream titles to independent French flicks. Be sure to make time for a tipple at the bar on the terrace; with its panoramic view that looks out over the Sacré-Coeur it's the perfect place for a post- or pre-film drink.
170 Boulevard de Magenta, 75010
+33 (0)1 4463 9698
cinemalouxor.fr

Inside out
Le Grand Rex comes with a courtyard view

2

Le Grand Rex, Bonne Nouvelle (2e)
Whole new world

Built in 1932, this art deco-style theatre is one of the largest cinemas in Europe and was designed to transport audiences into a world of fantasy. The main screening hall resembles a Mediterranean courtyard, complete with mock buildings and towers, while the ceiling is painted as a starry sky to create the impression of being in an open-air venue. In 1981 this much-loved theatre secured a place in the Mérimée register of historic monuments.

In addition to screening Hollywood blockbusters and classic films, Le Grand Rex puts on an impressive schedule of concerts. On a Saturday night you'll find its 2,650 seats packed with Parisians watching archive performances by musicians such as Ludovico Einaudi and James Morrison.
1 Boulevard Poissonnière, 75002
+33 (0)1 4508 9389
legrandrex.com

3

Le Champo, Latin Quarter (5e)
Film fix

This arthouse cinema is an institution of Paris film culture. It offers a mix of classic and contemporary, as well as retrospectives from the likes of Jacques Tati. For those partial to a late-night viewing, from midnight Les Nuits de Champo offers three films and breakfast for €15.
51 Rue des Écoles, 75005
+33 (0)1 4354 5160
lechampo.com

Watch this space

Rue Champollion in the Latin Quarter lays claim to a number of independent cinemas. Its Filmothèque revival house and indie cinema has a broad selection of nightly showings; if you're in Paris at the right time, check out one of its annual international film festivals.
lafilmotheque.fr

Paris on film

01 Last Tango in Paris, 1972: Bertolucci's cast of Marlon Brando and Maria Schneider is bound to seduce. As strangers the pair collide under the Bir-Hakeim Bridge and enter into a strictly anonymous nymphomaniac relationship. Paris itself stars as the erotic metropolis that we all know it to be.

02 Three Colours, 1993-1994: Although the brainchild of Polish director Krzysztof Kieslowski, this trilogy is quintessentially French. Each film is themed on one of the three hues of the French tricolour and plots the basics of French culture. The first – *Blue* – is set in Paris. Juliette Binoche laps in the Piscine Pontoise pool and strolls along the Rue Mouffetard street market.

03 Midnight in Paris, 2011: Paris's Latin Quarter stars in this film by Woody Allen. Follow writer Gil (Owen Wilson) as he time-travels every midnight into the city's 1920s arts scene. The Shakespeare and Company bookshop, Deyrolle taxidermy curiosity shop and the Notre Dame Cathedral add up to a charming route through the heart of the city.

Media round-up
Word on the street

❶
Magazines and newspapers
Read all about it

English editions are few and far between on Parisian newsstands so we've rounded up the best in French-language print to help guide you through your stay. To check the latest on the stock markets and take the pulse of the European business world, buy a copy of financial newspaper ❶ *Les Echos*. For a lighter and more city-centric focus opt for the tabloid ❷ *Le Parisien*; this publication, like its sister title *L'Équipe*, is one of the most sold newspapers in France.

A familiar title on international shelves is stalwart daily Berliner ❸ *Le Monde*, which has been in operation since 1944. ❹ *Le Guide Fooding* by *lefooding.com* is a yearly publication that uncovers the lesser-known restaurants, hotels and guesthouses the country over. And finally, the photo-rich weekly magazine ❺ *Paris Match* provides an in-depth take on both national and international news.

②
Newsstands, citywide
Off the rack

Ornate green news kiosks have been a feature of Parisian street corners for more than 150 years. Now joined by the JCDecaux chrome-and-glass equivalents built from the 1980s, these street-side newsstands account for more than 40 per cent of all printed media sold in the capital. Their presence is now protected by the City of Paris, which launched a campaign in 2013 to encourage residents to support these vendors.

All are dependable outposts for a daily dose of news and most stock good magazines. Kiosquier Jacky Goubert and his daughter Gaelle run the staunch establishment at 170 Boulevard Saint-Germain-des-Prés, 75006, between Café de Flore and Les Deux Magots in the 6th arrondissement. While a fine example of the new era of kiosk design can be found across from the Pompidou Centre on Place Edmond Michelet, 75004.

Radio

01 RFI: This highbrow current-affairs station at 89.0FM hosts daily news analysis and draws from its network of more than 400 correspondents worldwide, broadcasting in 13 languages across 62 countries.
rfi.fr

02 France Inter: Jump into most taxis and you'll probably hear the talk-heavy wavelengths of 87.8FM. The station is owned by public broadcaster Radio France and one of its most listened-to spots is the *Le 7/9* breakfast show.
franceinter.fr

03 France Culture: At 93.5FM is this cultural offering from Radio France, covering everything from philosophy to history, as well as literary readings.
franceculture.fr

04 NRJ: Paris-based commercial media giant NRJ Group first launched its radio station in 1981 in France and has since expanded to 18 countries. It plays the latest chart-topping tunes at 100.3FM.
nrj.com

Design and architecture
Create a scene

Exploring the City of Light is an architectural adventure like no other. It's a city that's full of design rules: Haussmann's boulevards, prescribed façades, regulated kiosks and sanctioned street signs. Here we'll guide you through some of these urban conventions and show you how they make Paris what it is today.

Along the way, of course, are architectural surprises aplenty. From the medieval Palais de la Cité to the gleaming towers of La Défense – via the host of modernist masters, art nouveau beauties and brutalist mass-housing projects that came in between – this section shows that Parisian architecture is far from standardised. Just take a look at the swooping lines and gleaming shells of two of the most dramatic recent builds – Jean Nouvel's Philharmonie de Paris and Frank Gehry's Fondation Louis Vuitton – and you'll see for yourself that the city's architects are certainly not hamstrung by any need to conform.

Contemporary
Here and now

①
Philharmonie de Paris, Parc de la Villette (19e)
Hitting the right note

Paris is used to architectural controversies but the furor that was seen around the opening of the city's brand new concert hall in 2015 was exceptionally heated. Lead architect Jean Nouvel pulled his name from the project and decried the authorities for mismanagement and failure to stick to contracts. The first year of the Philharmonie's history was therefore beset with unfinished business but visible MDF panelling and duct tape aside, the vision of this great hulk of culture is plain to see.

Approaching the spaceship-cum-whale of a structure is an astonishing experience and most importantly of all, music critics have unanimously lauded the qualities of the dazzling concert hall. Acoustically adjustable seating and stage conformation have left the world's lovers of classical music astounded.

221 Avenue Jean Jaurès, 75019
+33 (0)1 4484 4484
philharmoniedeparis.fr

Let it shine
Thousands of aluminium pieces cover the ceiling

2

Siège du Parti Communiste Français, Belleville (19e)
Brazilian beauty

Almost floating above the Colonel Fabien traffic island is a rare chance to see the work of a titan of architecture outside of his native Brazil; Oscar Niemeyer delivered his client a lyrical masterpiece while he was in exile after a military coup back home.

The French Communist Party Headquarters was completed in 1971 at a time when the party and its ideology was still a force to be reckoned with in the country. A six-storey boomerang-shaped office block forms a glass curtain that opens up over the district. The upturned bowl, which recalls Niemeyer's Brasilia parliament building, contains a central debating chamber that has a ceiling shimmering with aluminium. The furniture in the curved foyer was also designed by the architect.
2 Place du Colonel Fabien, 75019
+33 (0)1 4040 1212
pcf.fr

3

Musée du Quai Branly, Champ de Mars (7e)

What lies beneath

Designed by Jean Nouvel and completed in 2006, this is the most recent and architecturally striking of Paris's great museums. President Mitterrand planned a grand cultural complex for the site but the proposals were blocked by the wary residents of this prestigious neighbourhood. Nouvel responded with a simple but sophisticated structure.

Inside, some 3,500 objects from the indigenous cultures of Africa, Asia, Oceania and the Americas are housed in a beguiling arrangement that weaves through a sensorial plan.
37 Quai Branly, 75007
+33 (0)1 5661 7000
quaibranly.fr

4

Fondation Louis Vuitton, Boulogne (16^e^)

Setting sail

Frank Gehry's monument for Bernard Arnault's Louis Vuitton Foundation, opened in 2014, resembles a ship; its sails are visible beyond the Jardin d'Acclimatation in Bois de Boulogne Park. Built by Gehry as a "vessel symbolising the cultural calling of France", its winged structure was designed to reflect the passage of time, while the water cascading into the moat evokes the image of a ship in the surf. And the exhibitions that artistic director Suzanne Pagé puts together are just as spectacular as the architecture.
8 Avenue du Mahatma Gandhi, 75116
+33 (0)1 4069 9600
fondationlouisvuitton.fr

Shades of grey

Light and dark concrete panels cover the façade

5

Hôtel Fouquet's Barrière, Champs-Élysées (8e)
Past and present

In 2003, French architect and landscape designer Edouard François was charged with the task of reinterpreting this collection of seven buildings on the Avenue des Champs-Élysées, a challenge given the site's location on one of the most iconic and uniform boulevards in Paris. His solution? To replicate the original Haussmann façade but add a twist.

Grey bas-relief concrete panels of differing shades and sizes replaced the sandstone that is ubiquitous in the area. The ornamental window frames of the period were recreated but are "closed" instead of fitted with glass; the functional windows are now modern rectangular frames set at seemingly haphazard intervals across the façade. This clashing of styles demarcates the hotel as a modern build and cleverly hints at the revised floorplan within.
46 Avenue George V, 75008
+33 (0)1 4069 6000
lucienbarriere.com

Haussmann's redesign of the city

There is perhaps no other city that has been so affected by the vision of one man: Baron George-Eugène Haussmann, prefect of the Seine working under Napoleon III, was largely responsible for the Paris laid out before us today.

From 1853 to 1870 and beyond, Haussmann's plans cut straight boulevards and avenues through the city's medieval core and out into the communes that Napoleon III incorporated into Paris. Named after military victories and local dignitaries (Magenta, Sebastopol, La Fayette) they made up 85km of new roads that sliced up Paris – in the words of Émile Zola, like "the strokes of a sabre".

Beyond Haussmann and Napoleon's mission to cleanse the city and provide it with better circulation, many have speculated on the military intentions of this drastic urban rationalisation: wide, straight streets enabling the quick suppression of armed uprisings. Whether or not this theory is true, the quintessential Parisian boulevard with elegantly uniform façades, cornices and rooflines certainly quashed the Paris of old.

Make a statement

The Centre Pompidou's hi-tech design and industrial façade earned it notoriety – and sparked controversy. But from its exposed multicolour piping to its glass tubular staircase, it is an impressive and individual building to behold.
centrepompidou.fr

Pre-20th century
Step back through time

1
Palais de la Cité, Île de la Cité (1e)
Civic landmark

No site in Paris encapsulates the social and political history of France like the Palais de la Cité. This bewildering complex includes everything from fully functional law courts to a medieval prison. The site's most spectacular component? The 13th-century Sainte-Chapelle.
2 Boulevard du Palais, 75001
+33 (0)1 5340 6080
tourisme.monuments-nationaux.fr

2
Troubadour, Pigalle (9e)
Happy ending

Incongruously situated in the neoclassical quarter of Nouvelle Athènes, this is a rare example of the Troubadour architectural style that enjoyed brief popularity in the early 19th century. Despite its sophisticated façade of gothic arches, niches and intricate reliefs, this solitary rebel of a building was, until its closure in 1946, a brothel named Chez Christiane.
9 Rue de Navarin, 75009

3
Le Musée Jacquemart-André, Champs-Élysées (8e)
Art-full home

In the 19th century the city's aristocracy began constructing lavish mansions along the tree-lined Haussmann Boulevard in what was once the village of Monceau. Among them were Edouard André and his wife Nélie Jacquemart, who collaborated with architect Henri Parent to design a building for their extensive art collection, which they had spent 30 years amassing.

Time seems to have come to a halt within the gilded stucco walls of the mansion, which has been left intact since it was bequeathed to the Institut de France and opened to the public in 1913. As of that day its beautifully appointed rooms have been showcasing the city's finest private collection of masterpieces including Louis XIV furniture, frescoes by Giambattista Tiepolo and paintings by Rembrandt and Canaletto.
158 Boulevard Haussmann, 75008
+33 (0)1 4562 1153
musée-jacquemart-andre.com

OK, well, it's been lovely talking to you but now I must be off...

4

Palais Garnier, Opéra (9e)
Showy splendour

Le Corbusier described architect Charles Garnier's style as the "decor of the dead" but this opulent beaux art opera house is a masterpiece. It was commissioned by Napoleon in 1860 and later became one of the most expensive buildings of Haussmann's redesign (*see page 109*).

There are seats for 2,000 in the auditorium, which has a seven-tonne chandelier designed by Garnier; in 1896 one of its counterweights killed a member of the audience when it fell, a horrific event that made its way into the pages of Gaston Leroux's novel *Phantom of the Opera*.
Place de l'Opéra, 75009
+33 (0)1 4001 1850
operadeparis.fr

Art deco and modernism
Get the look

A fine art

Frescoes, paintings and sculptures abound

1

Palais de Chaillot, Trocadéro (16e)
Setting the stage

The sheer size and sumptuousness of this modernist structure – as well as its astonishing views of the Eiffel Tower – make it an art deco revelation. France's most prestigious performance space was completed in 1937 for the Paris Universal Exhibition by architects Léon Azéma, Jacques Carlu and Louis-Hippolyte Boileau.

The centrepiece is the Grand Foyer, lined with a series of triumphant *torchères* to make it a very grand affair. Huge murals painted by a host of artistic heavyweights including Paul Belmondo and Louis Billotey only add to the exuberance. Much of the painting and ubiquitous gold leaf has lost its art deco sheen but the state and crowdfunded restoration programme launched in 2015 should make the theatre the star of the show once more.
1 Place du Trocadéro, 75016
+33 (0)1 5365 3000
theatre-chaillot.fr

②

Lavirotte Building, Champ de Mars (7e)

Natural beauty

This private residence manages to stand apart from the ornamented set of art nouveau apartment buildings in the area; Jules Lavirotte's 1901 design won the prize for the best façade in the city that year.

Seven storeys with four bays are arranged with typical art nouveau asymmetry; Lavirotte wanted to create an imbalance and a movement in the building in contrast to its rigidly Haussmannian neighbours. With a lizard door handle and bulls heads and turtles as balcony fulcrums, the theme is a dedication to the fertility of nature. The upside-down phallus on the front door sets the tone.

29 Avenue Rapp, 75007

③

Folies Bergère, Grands Boulevards (9e)

Life and soul

The name Folies Bergère is synonymous with the most exuberant period of Parisian history. Opened in 1869, the music hall became the entertainment hub par excellence for the Belle Époque; in 1882 Édouard Manet painted "A Bar at the Folies Bergère" (*see page 77*) and the venue's reputation for providing the city with urban titillation was set.

In 2013 attention was paid to the structure of this venerable institution: the 1930 art deco façade was ravishingly restored, with gold leaf replacing original copper foil.

32 Rue Richer, 75009
+33 (0)1 4479 9860
foliesbergere.com

④

Hôtel Martel, Auteuil (16e)

One-man band

This private modernist mansion was built between 1926 and 1927 by architect Robert Mallet-Stevens, who also designed the five other houses on the street that now bears his name. Together this extraordinary ensemble forms a unique urban snapshot that can be found nowhere else in Paris.

Externally the building, which was designed as a home and workshop for sculptor brothers Joël and Jan Martel, has a complex terraced structure that is unified by a central cylindrical stairwell. Internally the stairs weave in different levels, rooms and studios making for ever-changing interior spaces.

10 Rue Mallet-Stevens, 75016

In with the new

Appearing in Paris at the end of the 19th century, art nouveau was a response to the artistic monotony of the Second Empire. Over 550 pieces can be seen at Musée 1900, adjoining Maxim's restaurant, encompassing art, fashion and furniture.
maxims-de-paris.com

Postwar design
Après-arms

Just the job
180,000 people work in this district

1
La Défense
Risky business

La Défense is Europe's largest purpose-built business district, measuring some 160 hectares. Its development on Paris's Axe Historique in 1958 – by the dedicated Public Establishment for Installation of La Défense government body – was aimed at supporting the French economy, expanding the city's limits and housing a booming postwar population; some 70,000 people live in the district today.

That same year one of the area's first buildings was built: The Center of New Industries and Technologies, a glass-fronted modernist exhibition hall designed by Jean de Mailly, covered the Place de la Concorde. In its wake came standardised towers that were 100 metres high and 24 metres wide on each side, including the Tour Nobel (today the Tour Initiale) and the Tour Europe. The height standard that governed these builds was quickly slackened and gave way to the 110-metre-high structure that is now a city icon: the Grande Arche.

This behemoth was built using more than 300,000 tonnes of glass and Italian carrara marble and was suspended over 30-metre-deep foundations and 12 pillars that each bear three times the weight of the Eiffel Tower. It was a huge project for its creator Johan Otto von Spreckelsen, a Danish professor of architecture whose previous projects were mainly churches on the outskirts of Copenhagen. Spreckelsen's plans were selected by president François Mitterand from among 424 submissions. It was inaugurated on 14 July 1989, the bicentenary of the storming of the Bastille, and rumour has it that during the ceremony Margaret Thatcher was trapped in the building's toilets, forcing UK security to break down the doors.

Spreckelsen did not live to see the Grande Arche finished – he died in 1987 – so the project was handed over to French architect Paul Andreu. The structure is undergoing renovations until 2017, as one in six of its marble tiles are said to have cracked due to the material's porosity.
La Grande Arche: 1 Parvis de la Défense, 92044

Mass housing

In 1965 the government of Charles de Gaulle began building *villes nouvelles* (new towns; places like Cergy-pontoise and Marne-la-Vallée) on the outskirts of Paris to deal with a postwar influx of immigrants and a regional population that had boomed from 6.6 to 9.2 million in 20 years. As a series of mundane and minimalist buildings rose, a small number of these vast swathes of land became playgrounds for experimental architects who wanted to rebel against the strictly functional mass housing built by their modernist predecessors.

Both the government and architects entertained, to a certain extent, the notion that an artistically complex and sophisticated urban design would have an equally sophisticating effect on its populace. But the result has been somewhat the opposite: the dystopian, brute concrete edifices produced communes that have been troubled by crime and isolation from the rest of the city. Until recently, many were all but dismissed as ambitious architectural follies and sociopolitical failures. But today, with a Paris that is forever spreading its frontiers, these *villes nouvelles* have gradually been integrated into the capital.

Most importantly these postmodern behemoths, many of which resemble George Orwell's Ministry of Truth more than urban paradises, have been rediscovered for their architectural wonder and held up as symbols of an ephemeral bygone era of design. They have entered the pantheon of architectural curios thanks to their magnificent eccentricity. Absurd as they may seem to be, they are worth the journey on the RER.

Veggie vernacular

Another ambitious housing project, the Choux de Créteil (Cabbages of Créteil) in Val-de-Marne was designed by architect Gérard Grandval so that each balcony resembled a leaf, creating the overall layered effect of a cabbage.
bnf.fr

2

Les Espaces d'Abraxas, Noisy-le-Grand

Three's a crowd

Catalan architect Ricardo Bofill's 1982 neoclassical building is, in Bofill's own words, "a metaphor, a theatrical space" that marks the creation of Noisy-le-Grand. Taking its design from the Greek Odeon and Roman amphitheatre, Les Espaces d'Abraxas is composed of three separate structures built on a symmetrical axis: the rectangular Palacio, the curved glass-fronted Théâtre and the ersatz triumphal Arc crowning the centre.

Bofill rejected practical modernist features, such as methods to maximise sunlight exposure, in favour of 11-storey Doric columns and temple-like pediments. But the prefabricated concrete forces a repetitive style. The result is a caricature-coliseum – home to 591 apartments – that critics have branded a post-modern in-joke at the expense of its residents.

Noisy-le-Grand, Seine-Saint-Denis

3

Les Arènes de Picasso, Noisy-le-Grand

Round in circles

Spanish architect Manuel Nuñez Yanowsky's 500-apartment Les Arènes is, in part, inspired by 18th-century architect Étienne-Louis Boullée's neoclassical concept of a cenotaph for Sir Isaac Newton: a three-tier circular mausoleum of impossible proportions. Built in 1985 around the Place Pablo-Picasso near Les Espaces, it is known for the 14-storey circular edifices on each end, towering over art deco-inspired arcades. Although Yanowsky intended them to resemble an overturned chariot, they're known among residents as "Les Camemberts".

Noisy-le-Grand, Seine-Saint-Denis

4

Les Tours Aillaud, Nanterre

Sky's the limit

Emille Aillaud's 18 multicoloured towers went up in 1977, west of the newly developed La Défense (*see page 113*). They are known as the "Tours Nuages" (Cloud Towers), so easily do they blend into the sky. A huge tiled serpent designed by artist Laurence Rieti marks the central path between the buildings; it takes its inspiration from Antoni Gaudí's mosaic salamander in Barcelona.

The 1,607-apartment complex has had more favourable reviews than most of its peers but one problem is cited time and again: the teardrop windows on the buildings are highly fragile and at €540 each have cost the council a small fortune.

Allé de l'Arlequin, 92000

5

Les Arcades du Lac et le Viaduc, Montigny le Bretonneux
Ahead of the curve

Described by Ricardo Bofill as "the Versailles of the people", this was the Catalan's first mass-housing project in France. It was completed in 1982 shortly before Les Espaces (*see page 115*) but the style is entirely different. Here Bofill has opted for light efficiency, creating mini squares of four-storey buildings on a symmetrical axis that echoes the quads of Oxford colleges.

Les Arcades joins the Viaduc: a six-building "viaduct" over an artificial lake, modelled on the Château de Chenonceau. Together they comprise 463 apartments that sit on top of an underground car park.
Sourderie, Montigny le Bretonneux

Design museums
Got it made

1

Pavillon de l'Arsenal, Arsenal (4e)
Urban information

This documentation centre opened in 1988 to exhibit past and present architectural projects in Paris. There is a permanent display of 1,000 documents, pictures and maps, as well as a digital model called "Paris Métropole 2020" developed with Google and JCDecaux.
21 Boulevard Morland, 75004
+33 (0)1 4276 3397
pavillon-arsenal.com

2

Galerie Kreo, Saint-Germain-des-Prés (6e)
State of the art

Since 1999, Clémence and Didier Krzentowski have invited the world's most talented designers to create pieces for them. In this 17th-century *hôtel particulier* are works from contemporary talents and rare pieces from 1950 to 1980.
31 Rue Dauphine, 75006
+33 (0)1 5310 2300
galeriekreo.com

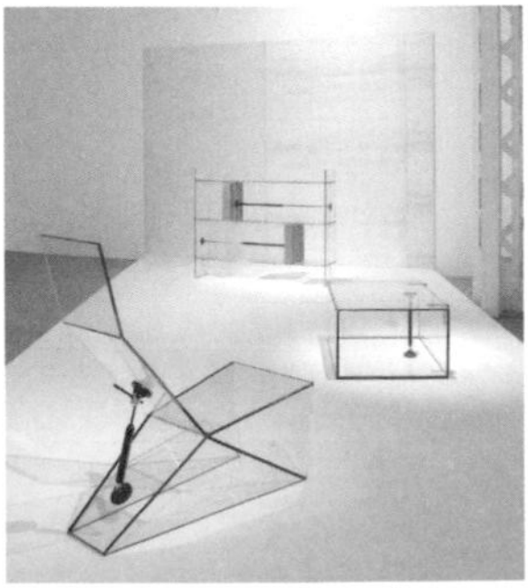

③
Cité de la Mode et du Design, Les Docks (13e)
Let's get together

This unique space dedicated to art, design and entertainment in a set of revamped warehouses on the Seine is a little difficult to classify. First there's the serpentine etched-glass tube snaking its way across the river-facing façade; for the best views of this Jakob + MacFarlane-designed structure you actually need to be on the opposite bank. On the first floor, the Art Ludique gallery presents a roster of exhibitions dedicated to "fun art": manga, comics, film, animation and video games. On the spacious wooden-deck rooftop there's the Moon Roof and Nüba bars and restaurants – come nightfall the latter turns into a thumping club dedicated to techno, house and hip-hop – and a garden designed by Michel Desvignes.

On any given day or night you'll find film screenings, pop-up shops, crossfit and yoga classes and food festivals. The IFM – Paris's school of fashion, textiles and design – also has its home here. It all makes for one of the most interesting mixed-use spaces dedicated to the creative industries in the city.
34 Quai d'Austerlitz, 75013
+33 (0)1 7677 2530
citemodedesign.fr

④
Jousse Entreprise, Saint-Germain-des-Prés (3e and 6e)
Postwar passion

Philippe Jousse helped pioneer the concept of furniture design as a serious art form. His gallery started as a stall at the Port de Clignancourt; today it champions young talent.
Furniture: 18 Rue de Seine, 75006
+33 (0)1 5382 1360
Art: 6 Rue Saint-Claude, 75003
+33 (0)1 5382 1018
jousse-entreprise.com

⑤
Cité de l'Architecture et du Patrimoine, Trocadéro (16e)
Building blocks

Inaugurated in 2007 by former president Nicolas Sarkozy, this is everything an architecture museum should be. Occupying the east wing of the Palais de Chaillot, the collection charts the structural, decorative and design delights of French architecture from medieval to modern and beyond.

The first level is devoted to gothic and renaissance edifices that define French heritage: life-sized models of Chartres Cathedral's doorways and other buildings' buttresses, domes and spires abound. Upstairs France's built beauty continues with a reconstruction of a section of Le Corbusier's Unité d'Habitation in Marseille. The modern gallery is the place to indulge in some architectural peeping: crouch down and join a miniature world of towers, housing estates and villas with the hundreds of beautifully made models on display.
1 Place du Trocadéro, 75116
+33 (0)1 5851 5200
citechaillot.fr

Street wise
Get to know Paris with miniature replicas

6

Maison La Roche, Auteuil (16e)
Modern marvel

The 16th arrondissement had its heydey in the interwar years when any self-respecting doctor, lawyer or indeed architect would need an address here for their studio. Little wonder therefore that along with the Haussmannian fineries of the haute bourgeoisie came the stripped-back designs of modernism and clients that could pay for them. The hemmed-in site meant that the architects had to use all of their spatial tricks while not straying from their newly perfected aesthetic purity.

Maison La Roche was built by Le Corbusier and Pierre Jeanneret in 1925. Today it's home to the Fondation Le Corbusier and design enthusiasts can trawl through an archive of more than 8,000 drawings and plans created by the late great architect.
8-10 Square du Docteur Blanche, 75016
+33 (0)1 4288 4153
fondationlecorbusier.fr

Retail
In the bag

1

Galeries Lafayette, Opéra (9e)
Talking shop

While it may seem strange to include a department store in a list of must-see venues, this is no ordinary shopping centre. Since its beginnings as a small haberdashery shop in 1893, Galeries Lafayette has been turned into a dazzling temple to retail.

A 43-metre-high dome – designed by architect Louis Majorelle and stained-glass artist Jacques Gruber – was installed to flood the gallery space with light. The art nouveau balconies were designed by decorator Louis Majorelle. The Galeries' heritage team offers free guided tours for groups of 10+.
40 Boulevard Haussmann, 75009
haussmann.galerieslafayette.com

All for one

Don't be fooled by its name: Publicis Drugstore is much more than a pharmacy. Step inside this glass-and-metal marvel on the Champs-Elysées and you'll find a bookshop, deli, restaurant and more. As well, of course, as a trusty medical store.
publicisdrugstore.com

2

Hermès, Saint-Germain-des-Prés (6e)
Swimmingly good design

An unassuming entrance from the street hides one of Paris's most extraordinary retail spaces. Converted from the 1930s Lutétia swimming pool by the RDAI architecture agency in 2010, Hermès' concept store is dominated by three nine-metre-tall ash huts that contain homeware and other brand fineries.

The art deco pool is a historic monument and its details have been lovingly preserved and restored; the original structure is allowed to breathe and at the same time it complements the contemporary huts. A feeling of sculpture, space and light make for a visit that is as cultural as it is commercial. The first level also hosts Hermès' prestigious tea room as well as a luxury stationery and bookshop put together by Swiss pen-and-pencil manufacturers Caran d'Ache.
17 Rue de Sèvres, 75006
+33 (0)1 4222 8083
hermes.com

City bridges

01 **Pont Neuf, Île de la Cité:** Paris's oldest bridge was a symbol of innovation when it was built by Henry IV in 1607; *neuf* means "new". It was the first bridge to cross the entire width of the Seine, have pavements and be made of stone rather than wood. The most modern touches of all are the viewing platforms and benches.

02 **Pont Mirabeau, Mirabeau/Javel:** This striking green bridge was constructed in 1896 by Paul Rabel. The piles on each end represent boats bearing four allegorical statues: Commerce and Abundance on one side, Navigation and the City of Paris on the other. Yet despite the neoclassical ornamentation the steel-iron body is pure art nouveau, making this a rare architectural blend.

03 **Pont Alexandre III, Champs-Élysées/ Invalides:** This bridge was built for the 1900 World's Fair by engineers Jean Résal and Amédée Alby. The 154-metre-long metallic structure presents four pylons, each topped with a gilded bronze Pegasus and a statue representing Arts, Sciences, Trading and Industry respectively.

Outdoor areas
Green retreats

1
Parc André Citröen, Javel (15ᵉ)
Reclaimed urban locale

When the industrial 15th arrondissement began to be encroached upon by residential development in the 1980s, the Citroën production plant was transformed into a two-hectare patch of greenery. A team of landscape architects lead by Gilles Clément and Alain Provost expanded this into a city oasis for nearby residents, capturing contemporary trends in landscaping.

The most commanding aspects of the park include a grassy expanse that extends from the banks of the Seine, featuring a tethered air balloon and two gargantuan greenhouses; one is now home to a eucalypt forest.
Rue Balard et Quai André Citroën

2
Unesco Headquarters, Champ de Mars (7ᵉ)
Thinking space

Osaka-born architect Tadao Ando's shrine to commemorate the 50th anniversary of Unesco, founded in 1945, is worth the short eastbound trek from the Eiffel Tower. Tucked in the shadows of the institution's soaring headquarters, within earshot of the patter of a Japanese stream, a solitary ramp leads to the circular tower that forms the centre of Ando's Meditation Space.

Made of granite stone that was sourced from Hiroshima in Japan, the space was designed to remind the world's delegates of the horror that transpired on that fateful August day (the same year Unesco was established) and to instill in visitors a sense of contemplative meditation. The tranquil courtyard is not only suited for taking a breather: it's also a good spot to mingle with global leaders.
7 Place de Fontenoy, 75352
+33 (0)1 4568 1000
unesco.org

Cemeteries

01 Catacombes de Paris, Montparnasse
More than 2,000 years of the city's history is embedded in labyrinths 20 metres below central Paris. Their origins go back to the 18th century when many Parisian cemeteries were shut down for sanitary reasons. Over the years roughly six million bodies were moved to these disused quarry galleries. Visitors can walk among the bones for a small fee.
catacombes.paris.fr

02 Cimetière du Montparnasse, Montparnasse
This 19-hectare graveyard is a sanctuary in the heart of Montparnasse, despite the tourists paying respect to icons such as Charles Baudelaire. Weave your way through the maple tree-lined alleys to explore its eclectic funerary architecture and be sure to see the grave of Tatiana Rachewskaïa – a Russian anarchist who committed suicide in 1910 – topped by Romanian sculptor Constantin Brancusi's "The Kiss".
3 Boulevard Edgar Quinet, 75014

03 Cimetière de Montmartre, Montmartre
At the foot of Montmartre sits the third-largest necropolis in Paris. Since 1825 it has been the resting place of this celebrated quarter's residents; among the modest carpenters and bakers you'll find shrines to musical and literary luminaries such as Hector Berlioz and Émile Zola. Look out for the bronze copy of Michelangelo's "Horned Moses" atop the tomb of financier Daniel Iffla.
20 Avenue Rachel, 75018

Transport
On the move

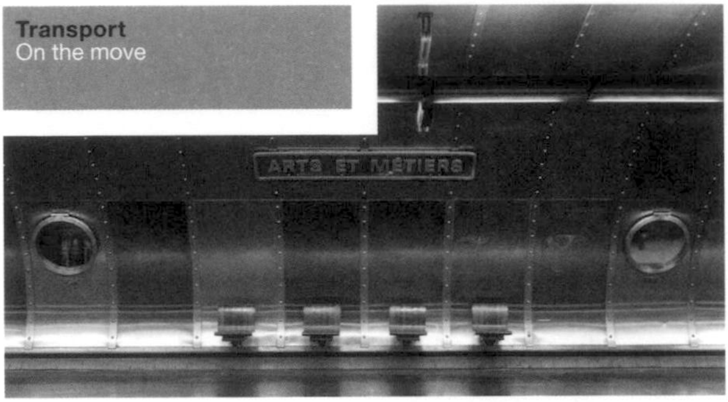

1
Arts et Métiers Métro, Arts et Métiers (3e)
Sea change

Clad in copper panels, the Arts et Métiers platform on Line 11 is a far cry from the classical white stops along the Metro. Inspired by Jules Verne's nautical vessel from *20,000 Leagues Under the Sea*, Belgian cartoon artist François Schuiten designed the station to feel as though you're stepping aboard a submarine.
Rue Réaumur, 75003

2
Palais Royal – Musée du Louvre Métro, Louvre (1er)
Dazzling romance

The Palais Royal stop on Place Colette was one of architect Hector Guimard's eight original Métro stops. The gaudy artwork by Jean-Michel Othoniel was installed in 2000 to celebrate its centenary. As an homage to love, Othoniel topped the arches with two crowns for day and night, representing the union of opposites.
Place Colette, 75001

3
Pont de Bir-Hakeim, Champ de Mars (15e)
Sky travel

The two-tier Pont de Bir-Hakeim was built across the Seine in the early 20th century and designed by architect Jean-Camille Formigé – the man behind, among other things, the sloping gardens below Sacré-Coeur.

Metro Line 6 uses the upper level of the steel bridge while vehicles, bicycles and pedestrians traverse the river between the city's 15th and 16th arrondissements on the lower level. The railway is supported by metal colonnades and a central arch that stands on the Île aux Cygnes. It's worth a visit to see the view of the Eiffel Tower and the statues and reliefs adorning the bridge.
Quai de Grenelle, 75015

④

Abbesses Métro, Pigalle (18e)

Under cover

The Abbesses Metro stop was constructed in 1913 and transferred from Hôtel de Ville in 1974. It is one of only three of Hector Guimard's wrought-iron-and-glass *édicule* entrances that survived the 1920s Paris-wide demolition of his work. Don't miss walking down the graffiti-covered walkway to see the Nord-Sud-style tiled platform too.

Place des Abbesses, 75018

Bleurgh! I'll need a different method of appearing cool and aloof
TABAC

Visual identity
Design of a city

①

Street signs, citywide

To the letter

Don't waste your time trying to navigate your way through Paris with postcodes: reading *les plaques de rues* is the way to go. Made up of white letters on ultramarine-blue nameplates, these signs were introduced in the city in 1847 and have remained unchanged ever since. Incidentally, only 2.6 per cent of them bear a woman's name. Old school, indeed.

②

Les Colonnes Morris, citywide

Play and display

With the increased popularity of plays, films and concerts in Paris in the mid-19th century, promotional material began taking over the city. The answer to this onslaught of advertising? Morris columns courtesy of French printer Gabriel Morris, who won the advertising concession in 1868. Thus were born the dark-green cylinders seen throughout Paris today.

③

Carotte tobacco signs, citywide

In good shape

Since 1906, tobacconists across France have been obliged to display these red carrot-like signs above their shops due to a government decision to keep track of all tobacco sale points. The name originates from the *carrote de tabac* – a carrot-shaped roll of tobacco leaves sold since the days of Louis XIV – though many still think it derives from the practice of placing a chunk of carrot into tobacco boxes to keep leaves fresh.

In 2014 thousands of Parisian tobacconists dumped four tonnes of carrots at the doors of parliament in opposition to proposed neutral-packaging laws.

④

Kiosques à journaux, citywide

Read all about it

These ubiquitous newsstands began to flourish on Parisian pavements in the late 19th century. Selling a range of publications, from daily newspapers and satirical cartoons to international magazines, they are considered fine ambassadors of print journalism (*see page 105*). Here's a tip: they don't appreciate being confused with the tourism office.

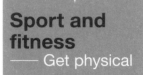

Sport and fitness
— Get physical

Paris isn't a particularly sports-oriented city, perhaps because you can stay fit just walking and cycling around the compact central arrondissements. Popular recreational pastimes tend towards the serene: a game of pétanque next to a centuries-old palace, a punt around a lake in a lush park or even a whirl on the ice rink in front of the beautiful Hôtel de Ville.

But for those who prefer to break a sweat in more traditional fashion we've selected our favourite tennis courts and pools, many of which are historic institutions in themselves. In Paris aesthetics are as important as function – and who doesn't like to admire a little art deco design or a 17th-century orangerie while chasing the black line in the pool or a tennis ball around the court?

If you simply must stay indoors, we've listed the sports centres and hotel gyms that get our tick of approval too. And finally, you'll find barbers and hairdressers to ensure that you're primped and preened to Parisian standards.

Swimming
Dive right in

①
Piscine Pontoise, Latin Quarter (5e)
Stroke of genius

The brown-brick exterior of this sports complex gives nothing away about the beauty that lies within: a pool covered by a glass roof and surrounded by tiers of individual art deco-style changing rooms. There's also a gym, sauna, salon, fitness classes and squash courts.

Single-day entry to the pool costs €4.80, evening entry (from 20.00) is €11.10 and a single gym pass is €21.60. Other highlights include the extended opening hours from 07.00 until 23.45.
19 Rue de Pontoise, 75005
+33 (0)1 5542 7788
carilis.fr/centre/espace-sportif-pontoise

2

Piscine Molitor, Porte Molitor (16e)
Birthplace of the bikini

This art deco swimming complex with a 33-metre-long indoor pool and a 46-metre-long lido was opened to the public in 1929 by Olympic swimmers Aileen Riggin Soule and Johnny Weissmuller. This was the place where Louis Réard unveiled the first bikini in 1946 and also where the topless sunbathing revolution was born.

In 1989 the space was abandoned but in 2014 the pools reopened as part of the luxury hotel MGallery. Entry for an early-morning swim and breakfast buffet at chef Julien Mercier's restaurant starts from €45.
13 Rue Nungesser et Coli, 75016
+33 (0)1 5607 0850
mltr.fr

3

Piscine Joséphine Baker, Port de la Gare (13e)
Seine-side swimming

This sophisticated swimming pool and fitness centre is built on a barge docked on the Seine near the Bibliothèque François Mitterrand. Architect Robert de Busni designed the glass-and-aluminium floating structure that incorporates an eco-friendly filter mechanism to fill the pool with water from the river.

In addition to the 25-metre-long main pool and the paddling pool for kids, the facility has a sauna. There is also a range of fitness classes on offer, including pilates and aqua-cycling. On warm days visitors havc access to a 500 sq m rooftop that has sunloungers with views over the Seine; it's a lovely place for a spot of post-exercise relaxation. Be warned, though: the pool can get extremely crowded at peak times.
Quai François Mauriac, 75013
+33 (0)1 5661 9650
carilis.fr/centre/piscine-josephine-baker

I've brought my rubber ring in case my doggy paddle fails me

Haircare and grooming

01 L'Humaine Comédie Yuji, Bourse: Japanese hairdressers Yuji Ishii and Jennifer Duniau are the creative talents behind this excellent hair salon opposite Square Louvois. The tiled floors and wooden shelves remain from the book-and-antiques shop that used to occupy the space.
humainecomedie-yuji.com

02 22 Rue de Verneuil, Saint-Germain-des-Prés: This salon is just a short walk from Serge Gainsbourg's house in the 7th arrondissement. It only has two staff members so bookings are essential. Pauline Finet cuts and Wanig Le Gall colours, while their two pet bulldogs watch the shop.
22ruedeverneuil.com

03 David Mallett, Montorgueil Quarter: In 2002, Australian David Mallett moved to Paris with 11 years' experience as a hairdresser. Today he is one of the city's most sought-after stylists, having worked for Karl Lagerfeld, Dior and French *Vogue*. His salon is in a lofty 17th-century apartment in the 2nd arrondissement.
david-mallett.com

04 Le Hammam at Grande Mosquée de Paris, Latin Quarter: The Grande Mosquée de Paris, which was built between 1922 and 1926, includes a traditional hamam. After a bath, scrub and massage we recommend enjoying a mint tea and some North African pastries on the patio.
restaurantauxportesdelorient.com

Outdoor activities
Exercise en plein air

1

Pétanque, citywide
Rolling in style

In the city's parks and squares you'll see groups playing this game that originated in the south of France, often over drinks. It can be played wherever there's a patch of lawn. The goal is to throw steel balls as close as possible to a wooden ball known as a *cochonnet*. Pétanque sets can be hired from delivery service Paris Ma Belle.
+33 (0)6 6752 6290
parismabelle.com

2

Ice-skating at Hôtel de Ville, Le Marais (4e)
Winter wonderland

From mid-December until March the square in front of the grand city hall undergoes an icy transformation. The 1,365 sq m rink is free and skates can be rented for €6. Regular events to look out for include ice-hockey matches and figure-skating shows. It's especially beautiful at night when the building is lit up.
Place de l'Hôtel de Ville, 75004

Tennis and squash

01 Jardin du Luxembourg, Saint-Germain-des-Prés: Playing tennis in these pretty gardens – surrounded by the church of Saint-Sulpice and the Luxembourg Palace – is a unique experience. And it's no secret so wake up early to book a court; 10 sessions will cost you €90.
+33 (0)1 4325 7918

02 Squash et Jeu de Paume, Trocadéro: This club in the 16th arrondissement offers four squash courts, a gym and a bar-restaurant. It is also one of the last venues in Paris to offer the centuries-old racquet game *Jeu de Paume*; one hour on a court is €30 per person. For squash, if you stop by during the week in off-peak time, the fee for an hour is €15.
squashjeudepaume.com

03 Le Fonds des Princes, Boulogne: This tennis centre is a little further out from the city centre in the 16th arrondissement. The five courts straddle the world-famous stadium that hosts the French Open. Pending the stadium's expansion, the courts are available for public use; an hour will set you back €9.
+33 (0)1 4651 1753

Sports centres and gyms
We can work it out

1

Centre sportif Jules Ladoumègue, Parc de la Villette (19e)
All together now

It's a bit of a hike from the centre of Paris but this cutting-edge and comprehensive sports centre is worth the travel time. Facilities include two outdoor and six indoor tennis courts (hopefully the bright red ceiling won't put you off your game), a dance studio and spaces for basketball, football and squash.

There is also a 150 sq m gym with all the equipment necessary to break a sweat. And to add a little variety to your fitness regime, why not try the climbing wall?
37 Route des Petits Ponts, 75019
+33 (0)1 4915 0878
equipement.paris.fr/centre-sportif-jules-ladoumegue-3080

Hotel gyms

01 Prince de Galles, Champs-Élysées: This five-star hotel fitness centre ticks all the boxes. Guests can work out around the clock and book personal training sessions. Plus the ritzy Wellness Suite overseen by Olivier Lecocq offers massages, beauty treatments and a hamam for post-session pampering.
princedegallesparis.com

02 Le Bristol, Champs-Élysées: Hotel guests can access this well-appointed fitness centre from 06.30 to 22.30. Personal training sessions are also available. A highlight is the indoor, teak-decked swimming pool with views of the Eiffel Tower and Sacré-Coeur (*see page 20*).
lebristolparis.com

②
CMG Sports Club, citywide
In and out

Guests can purchase single-day passes for any of the 22 CMG Sports Club locations across the city. Each outpost offers slightly different facilities; there are squash courts at Montparnasse and aquatic classes at Défense Coupole, for example. No matter which branch you choose, the equipment is always hi-tech.
cmgsportsclub.com

Wherever you will go

Ideal for frequent flyers, L'Usine offers members access to its Paris, Brussels and Geneva outposts. Its multi-level location in the 2nd arrondissement offers about 70 classes per week as well as use of the spa.
usineopera.com

Park life
Paddle and pedal power

Island paradise — Lac Daumesnil has two isles to explore

①
Bois de Vincennes, Bercy (12e)
Pretty punting

This huge park on the eastern edge of the city is one of the most popular spots for boating and all-round R&R. From €12.20 per hour you can hire one of the boats moored at the northwestern tip of Lac Daumesnil (a five-minute walk from the Porte Dorée métro stop). Look out for the neoclassical pavilion on the edge of the Île de Reuilly.

Rent a ride from Cyclorama on the edge of the lake; it will cost you €12 for half a day. From there either pedal northeast to the 14th-century Château de Vincennes or spend the afternoon tracing the 13km of bicycle lanes.
Bois de Vincennes, 75012
cycloramaevents.fr

②
Bois de Boulogne, Boulogne (16e)
Boats and bikes

At the northern tip of Lac Inférieur you can rent a traditional wooden *canot* (dinghy) for €10 per hour. A trip around the lake takes an hour (longer if you stop for lunch at Le Chalet des Iles on the central islet).

For those who feel like stretching their legs, bikes are available for hire from Paris Cycles on the mini-roundabout next to the Jardin d'Acclimatation. There are 15km of cycling routes, the course around the Hippodrome de Longchamp being the most popular. You can also take a guided cycle tour.
14 Chemin de Ceinture du Lac Inférieur, 75016
+33 (0)1 4288 0469
chalet-des-iles.com

Cycling
Pedal pushing

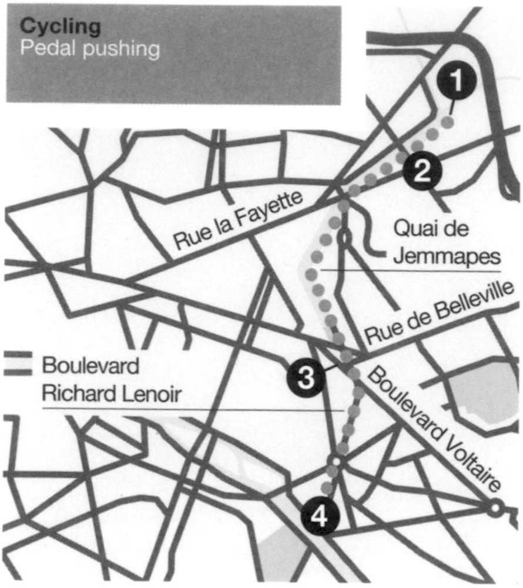

By 2020 Paris aims to double the length of its bicycle lanes from the current network of 700km to at least 1,400km; more than €150m will be invested in the project and it is predicted that cycling will account for 15 per cent of all trips made in the city. Vélib, a bike-sharing scheme, was introduced in 2007 and now provides more than 20,000 bikes with docking stations about every 300m. To avoid traffic, explore the central arrondissements on Sunday mornings or stick to the isolated bicycle-only lanes in the parks, canals and outer neighbourhoods.

1

Canal Saint-Martin
Canalside route

STARTING POINT: 7 Quai de Metz, 75019
DISTANCE: 6km

Collect a bike from the ❶ *Quai de Metz Vélib* station and head northwest towards the junction of Canal de l'Ourcq and Canal Saint-Denis. Here the two waterways join together and flow into Canal Saint-Martin. Head south, sticking to the right-hand side along the protected cycle path.

It won't be long before you reach the ❷ *Rue de Crimée* bridge; when you do, follow the cycle path left and then right around the junction. After about 3km of pedalling alongside the water you'll notice that the canal disappears at ❸ *Boulevard Jules Ferry*. This is the beginning of the Richard Lenoir tunnel, which was built in 1860 to conceal the waterway.

Continue down past Place de la Bastille, where the Bastille prison stood until it was stormed and destroyed during the French Revolution. The water will re-emerge as Bassin de l'Arsenal and flow into the ❹ *Seine River*. Finish your bicycle ride here, using the docking station along Quai de la Rapée to your right.

Running routes
Need for speed

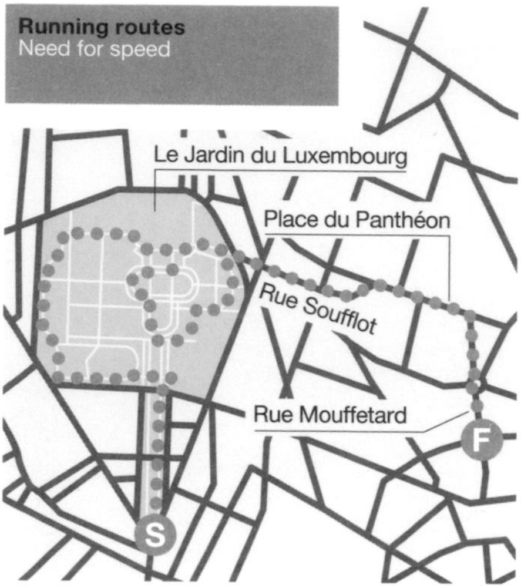

1

The Latin Quarter
Sights for sore eyes

DISTANCE: 4km
GRADIENT: Flat
DIFFICULTY: Easy
HIGHLIGHTS: The neoclassical cluster of architecture around the Panthéon
BEST TIME: Afternoon
NEAREST MÉTRO: Port-Royal station

Start your run at the green gates opening onto the slim grassy strip that is Jardin Marco Polo, with Fontaine de l'Observatoire at the entrance. Pass around this centrepiece and make a beeline for Jardin du Luxembourg straight ahead. Exit at the Esplanade Gaston-Monnerville, cross the road and enter Jardin du Luxembourg through the open gate to your right.

Take a hard left and loop around the outside through the chestnut trees passing the carousel, tennis courts and Palais du Luxembourg. Complete a full lap and head back up the centre strip towards the palace again. After passing the pond take a right up the stairs and exit the park towards the Panthéon.

Navigate your way around the roundabout and pass to the left of the Panthéon with Bibliothèque Sainte-Geneviève on your left. This neoclassical church is the burial place for French heroes including Voltaire, *The Three Musketeers* author Alexandre Dumas and French resistance heroine Geneviève de Gaulle-Anthonioz.

At the next block turn right down Rue Descartes; Ernest Hemingway once lived at number 39. Near Place de la Contrescarpe the street turns into Rue Mouffetard. The top end is a hub of crêperies and raclette restaurants and further down the cobbled lane is a selection of the area's best butchers, fromageries and *caves à vin* (wine cellars). Finish your run at the end of the street, walking back to stock up on wine and cheese.

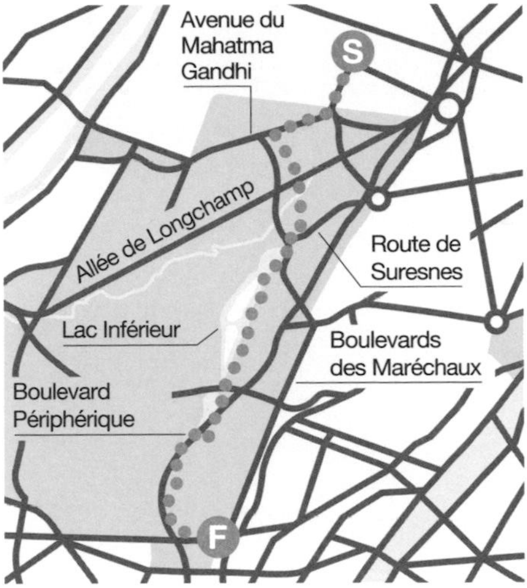

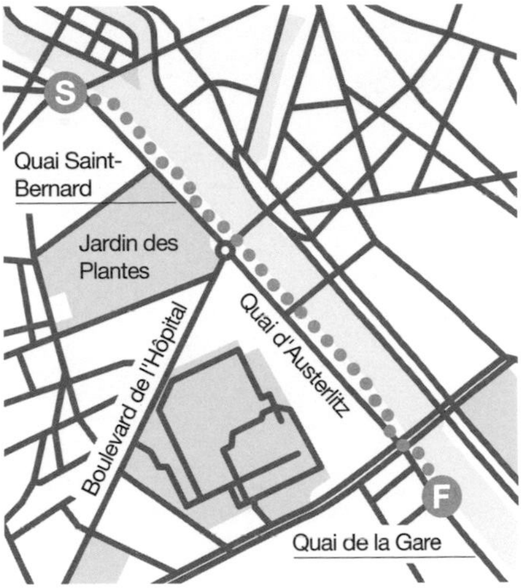

②
Bois de Boulogne
Park life

DISTANCE: 5km
GRADIENT: Flat
DIFFICULTY: Moderate
HIGHLIGHTS: No matter the season, the park's dense foliage is always beautiful
BEST TIME: Morning
NEAREST MÉTRO: Les Sablons

Begin along Boulevard des Sablons from the corner of Avenue Charles de Gaulle. After three short blocks, Jardin d'Acclimatation will be on your right. This children's amusement park opened as a zoo in 1860 as part of Napoleon III's mission to remodel the gardens of Paris. Follow the park's grounds around to your right and you'll see the silhouette of the Fondation Louis Vuitton. Designed by Frank Gehry, the building's sails are made from 13,500 sq m of glass that was manufactured in a custom-built furnace.

Next head across the pedestrian crossing, turn right and after just 10 metres turn left onto a trail towards Porte Dauphine. Continue along this track until you reach the intersection road. Cross at the pedestrian crossing and take a sharp right followed by a sharp left away from the road. Back on a woodland track you'll soon cross a small stream; keep running south along the paved footpath.

Once on Route de Suresnes turn right and cross the roundabout to run along the left bank of Lac Inférieur. Follow the lakeside track past the small ferry terminal. Shortly after, go up the rugged stairs and along the cycle path crossing the intersecting road. Continue down towards the Hippodrome d'Auteuil, looping up around the grandstands and then taking the path to your left. Follow the border of the jockey club along Route d'Auteuil aux Lacs, which will soon land you at the Porte d'Auteuil métro entrance: a good place to end your run.

③
Quartier de la Gare
River running

DISTANCE: 2km
GRADIENT: Flat
DIFFICULTY: Easy
HIGHLIGHTS: The riverside views and the sculpture park
BEST TIME: Morning or afternoon
NEAREST MÉTRO: Jussieu

This run starts outside the Institut du Monde Arabe in the 5th arrondissement and proceeds along the Seine south into the 13th arrondissement. It finishes near the Piscine Joséphine Baker and P7 restaurant so you can follow up with a swim and lunch.

Begin where Boulevard Saint-Germain meets Pont de Sully (the bridge). Look for the entrance that leads from the street down to the river and Jardin Tino-Rossi. After a hundred metres or so the winding pathway will lead you to the start of the Musée de la Sculpture en Plein Air, a park featuring about 50 artworks by artists such as Constantin Brancusi and Emile Gilioli.

As you approach the Pont d'Austerlitz bear right to take the path leading up and away from the water. Turn left at the intersection to return back to the Seine and pass under the bridge. Continue on under the Pont Charles de Gaulle and past the graffitied Cité de la Mode et du Design. When you pass under Pont de Bercy, you're near the end. Look for the parked barges and you'll spot the pool and the restaurant.

Where to buy

Decathlon (*decathlon.fr*) and GO Sport (*go-sport.com*) are France's biggest sports chains. There are also Adidas (*adidas.fr*) and Nike (*nike.com/fr*) megastores on the Champs-Élysées.

Walks
Find your own Paris

It only takes two hours to cross Paris on foot (from east to west or north to south) so it's an extremely walkable city. There's simply no better way of appreciating the myriad historic and cultural sites, art galleries, boutique sellers and lively bistros than by getting out among them. The tough part can be honing your focus. Here we've lent a helping hand by curating a selection of urban walks that will introduce you to the highlights of five of our favourite neighbourhoods.

NEIGHBOURHOOD 01

Le Marais
Paris of the past

Le Marais, which spans two arrondissements, is full of remarkable buildings of historical and architectural significance. Today the 3rd arrondissement, on and around Rue de Bretagne, is a see-and-be-seen quarter featuring galleries, high-end boutiques, smart cafés and chic cocktail bars; the 4th arrondissement, between Place des Vosges and Centre Pompidou, is slightly more touristy.

The Jewish quarter has been here for centuries, clustered around Rue des Rosiers. However, in recent years commercialism has been infringing on its traditional bakeries and delis at an alarming rate. Further west is the gay neighbourhood, from Rue Vieille du Temple, along Rue Sainte-Croix de la Bretonnerie to Rue du Temple, where bars and clubs display rainbow flags.

Although fashionable now, Le Marais was farmland in the 12th century. The wealthy moved in during the 17th century when Henri IV built Place des Vosges. After the court was transferred to Versailles it became a mercantile quarter. The interwoven streets were spared Haussmann's bulldozers but fell victim to ruin until more recent restorations, notably under General de Gaulle's culture minister (and novelist) André Malraux. Today the most well-heeled *hôtels particuliers* (private mansions) have been turned into museums: the Hôtel Salé hosts the Picasso Museum and the Hôtel Carnavalet is now home to the Musée Carnavalet.

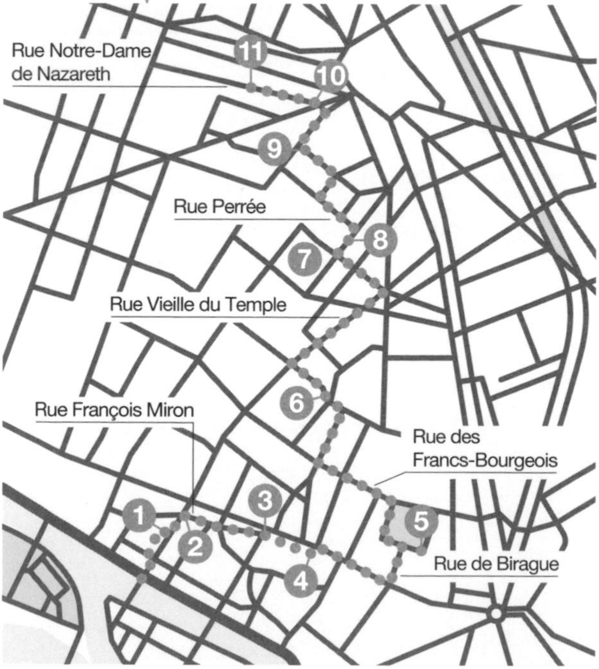

Cobbled classics
Le Marais walk

Start from the Seine and wander up Rue des Barres, a charming cobbled slope. Take a right into the narrow Rue du Grenier sur l'Eau to Rue du Pont Louis-Philippe and seek out (1) *Papier Plus* for paper goods and coloured pencils. Wander north until you reach Rue François Miron, then turn right: you'll notice the façades of Maison à l'Enseigne du Faucheur and Maison à l'Enseigne du Mouton, two 14th-century

Getting there

The closest Metro stops to start your walk are Pont Marie (Line 7) or Saint-Paul (Line 1); there are also Vélib' bike stations nearby. You'll end up near Temple (Line 3) but République is just beyond it with handy access to Lines 3, 5, 8, 9 and 11.

architectural marvels ribbed with exposed wood beams. Then pop into the colourful 2 *Izraël* to pick up spices and dried fruit from this family-run bazaar. Continue along Rue François Miron and you'll spot photographs through a street-side vitrine; glimpse into the 3 *Maison Européenne de la Photographie*, whose entrance is around the corner.

When Rue François Miron becomes Rue Saint-Antoine, find 4 *Fromagerie Laurent Dubois*, located next to a baroque Italian church. There you can sample a fruity *comté* or a *pélardon chèvre*. Turn off Rue Saint-Antoine onto Rue de Birague and emerge into Place des Vosges. Built for Henry IV, it features manicured greenery and refined stone buildings.

On the southeastern side is the lavishly furnished 5 *Maison de Victor Hugo*. The author of *Les Misérables* lived here from 1832 to 1848 but the building dates back to the early 17th century. It's a moody and evocative dwelling that doubtless fuelled Hugo's often dark narratives. Around the rest of the porticoed square are quaint cafés and restaurants, ideal for a leisurely stop. Leave the square by the more touristy and bustling Rue des Francs-Bourgeois. Afterwards turn up Rue Payenne and peek into the courtyard of the Institut Suédois, which has a gallery and café. If you're looking for sugary treats then 6 *Méert*, around the corner, has prettily wrapped biscuits and sweets.

Next find Rue Vieille du Temple for some shopping. The boutiques here are fashion favourites: separates at Le Mont Saint-Michel and designer gems at French Trotters. There's also Yvon Lambert, an excellent art book/magazine shop, and Breizh Café (111), an *épicerie* with specialities from Brittany. Then head north to Rue de Bretagne and turn left. Pick up lunch at 7 *Marché des Enfants Rouges*, named for the uniforms worn at the neighbouring orphanage in the 17th century. Today food stands – from Japanese bentos to savoury crêpes – are perfect for a quick bite.

Once sated, check out Parisian watchmaker 8 *March Lab* and then take a left on Rue du Forez to wander past the cast-iron-and-glass behemoth structure of Carreau du Temple, a former indoor market that's now an event space. Grab a coffee, made on a futuristic Kees van der Westen machine, at 9 *Fondation Café*; if it's a sunny day head for the tiny terrace. Nip into the galleries on Rue Notre-Dame de Nazareth, notably the pocket-sized 10 *MDM Gallery*, which shows up-and-coming Brazilian artists. Finish off the walk at 11 *Galerie Derouillon*, which hosts colourful and quirky artwork, such as the beguiling sculptures of Roman Moriceau.

Address book

01 Papier Plus
9 Rue du Pont Louis-Philippe, 75004
+33 (0)1 4277 7049
papierplus.com

02 Izraël
30 Rue François Miron, 75004
+33 (0)1 4272 6623

03 Maison Européenne de la Photographie
5/7 Rue de Fourcy, 75004
+33 (0)1 4478 7500
mep-fr.org

04 Fromagerie Laurent Dubois
97-99 Rue Saint-Antoine, 75004
+33 (0)1 4887 1710
fromageslaurentdubois.fr

05 Maison de Victor Hugo
6 Place des Vosges, 75004
+33 (0)1 4272 1016
maisonsvictorhugo.paris.fr

06 Méert
16 Rue Elzévir, 75003
+33 (0)3 2057 0744
meert.fr

07 Marché des Enfants Rouges
39 Rue de Bretagne, 75003
+33 (0)6 2052 3590
marchedesenfantsrougesfr.com

08 March Lab
50 Rue Charlot, 75003
+33 (0)1 7557 9390
march-lab.com

09 Fondation Café
16 Rue Dupetit-Thouars, 75003

10 MDM Gallery
6 Rue Notre-Dame de Nazareth, 75003
+33 (0)9 5459 2377
mdmgallery.com

11 Galerie Derouillon
38 Rue Notre-Dame de Nazareth, 75003
+33 (0)9 8062 9265
galeriederouillon.com

NEIGHBOURHOOD 02

Canal Saint-Martin

Waterway wander

The past decade has seen a transformation of the 10th arrondissement in the city's northeast. New bars, bistros and cafés can be found along Place de la République and Place Sainte-Marthe. Cutting-edge independent retailers such as La Trésorerie and Centre Commercial have set up shop, while the once-dilapidated Haussmann homes have become desirable dwellings for young professionals. Despite gentrification ploughing through the neighbourhood, the small-scale makers and sellers, such as Atelier 46 barber, have endured.

Arguably the best place to explore this blend of old and new is the area surrounding the tree-lined stretch of Canal Saint-Martin. Commissioned by Napoleon at the beginning of the 19th century, the canal was built to supply fresh water to inhabitants in the east. Its connection with Canal Saint-Denis and Canal de l'Ourcq in the north and the Seine in the south made it into an important transportation artery. This 4.5km stretch took 20 years to complete and has since undergone several renovations, including having almost half of its length sunk underneath Boulevard Richard-Lenoir. Fortunately it survived the threat of closure when boat traffic declined in the 1960s. The industrial blocks and mills lining the waterway are all but gone but the nine locks and pedestrian bridges still stand, adding historic charm to this modish quarter.

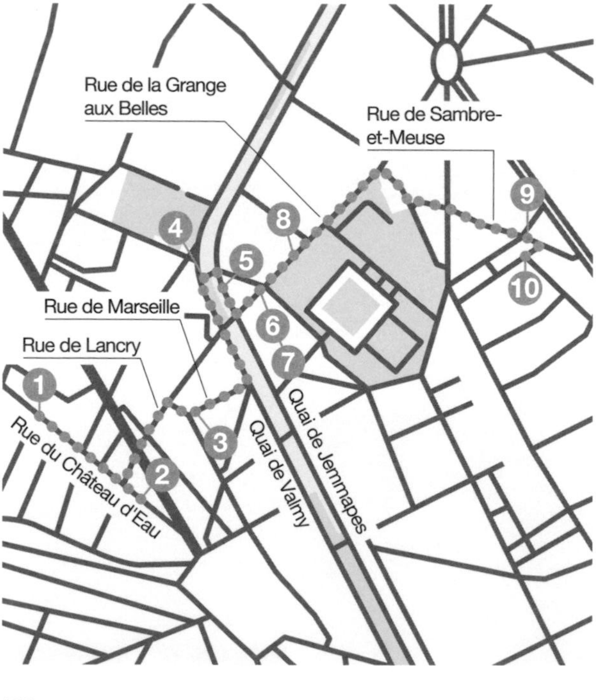

Canal calling

Canal Saint-Martin walk

Start your walk on Rue du Château d'Eau at ❶ *Marché Saint-Martin*. This recently renovated market is a good place to sample cheese, German ham and chocolates from Der Tante Emma-Laden. Turn right after exiting and continue down Rue du Château d'Eau until you reach the art deco-inspired exteriors of ❷ *La Trésorerie*. Inside, an impressive selection of homeware includes Gien tableware, Iris

Hantverk brushes and Sassi leather picnic bags.

Some pastry sampling is up next. Turn left out of La Trésorerie and take your first right onto Rue de Lancry. Cross busy Boulevard de Magenta and continue along Rue de Lancry. Turn down the third street to your right and you'll see the golden lettering of a century-old boulangerie straight ahead. Inside ❸ *Du Pain et des Idées*, mirrored walls and golden trimmings are a grand backdrop to the baked delicacies on offer. The fig tarts are hard to pass up. Afterwards round the corner to the right and peer through the bakery's pale-blue door to see the bakers at work. Continue on; you'll pass a healthy selection of retail outlets including the shopping mecca Centre Commercial. When you come across a light-pink primary school, take this as your cue to veer left; walk along the canal to Square des Récollets. Climb the stairs of the ❹ *Passerelle Bichat Bridge*; it dates back to the 1800s. The pavement and grass lining the waterway swarms with picnickers on summer evenings.

Cross the bridge and walk back in the direction you came, passing vintage shop 5 *Loulou Les Âmes Arts* on the left. Peek inside at the collection of berets perched above historical photographs of Paris. Exit and take your first left, venturing up towards the greenery of 6 *Bleuet Coquelicot*. Twice a week owner Tom des Fleurs fills his shop with fresh and unusual bunches. "People come to buy flowers, adopt a plant or share a coffee or wine," he says.

If you're in need of a pick-me up, stop in next door at café 7 *Ten Belles*, the brainchild of renowned French barista Thomas Lehoux. Spy out something tasty on the menu if you've still the appetite: the chef is Anna Trattles, formerly of St John restaurant in London. Continue up Rue de la Grange aux Belles. On the border of the hospital grounds to your right you'll see 8 *Chapelle Saint-Louis*. Henry IV laid the first stone here in 1607. After several minutes of walking uphill, follow the hospital boundaries around to your right.

Walk through Square Juliette Dodu and look up to your left at the antiquated stone walls of the bordering houses. Exit the square and turn left onto Rue de Sambre-et-Meuse. Cross Avenue Claude Vellefaux and continue until you see Rue Sainte-Marthe branching off to your right. This quaint cobbled street has come into its own in the past few years; Parisians come here from far and wide to sample its food-and-drink offerings. Before you settle down for dinner, whet the appetite with an opening drink at 9 *Palissade* on Rue de Sambre-et-Meuse, an informal and lively cocktail bar. Our pick from the menu is El Verde: a lemon and mezcal concoction.

Walk down Rue Sainte-Marthe. Chef Romain Tischenko of Top Chef fame co-owns two haunts here; La Cave à Michel (*see page 30*) and 10 *Le Galopin* a little further down the road. You've had a long walk so we recommend heading to the latter for a seven-course tasting menu. Tischenko's brother and business partner Maxime runs the kitchen and while portions are petite, the farm-fresh ingredients are top-notch.

Getting there

Jacques Bonsergent Metro station on Line 5 is a three-minute walk from the starting point. Alternatively, Strasbourg Saint-Denis on Lines 4, 8 and 9 is a seven-minute walk or Château d'Eau on Line 4 is a five-minute walk.

Address book

01 Marché Saint-Martin
33 Rue du Château d'Eau, 75010
+33 (0)1 4885 9330

02 La Trésorerie
11 Rue du Château d'Eau, 75010
+33 (0)1 4040 2046
latresorerie.fr

03 Du Pain et des Idées
34 Rue Yves Toudic, 75010
+33 (0)1 4240 4452
dupainetdesidees.com

04 Passerelle Bichat Bridge
Near Rue des Récollets, 75010

05 Loulou Les Âmes Arts
104 Quai de Jemmapes, 75010
+33 (0)1 4200 9139

06 Bleuet Coquelicot
10 Rue de la Grange aux Belles, 75010
bleuetcoquelicot.fr

07 Ten Belles
10 Rue De La Grange Aux Belles, 75010
+33 (0)1 4240 9078
tenbelles.com

08 Chapelle Saint-Louis
12 Rue de la Grange aux Belles, 75010
+33 (0)1 4249 9223

09 Palissade
36 Rue de Sambre-et-Meuse, 75010
+33 (0)1 8356 1846
palissade.biz

10 Le Galopin
34 Rue Sainte-Marthe, 75010
+33 (0)1 4206 0503
le-galopin.com

NEIGHBOURHOOD 03

South Pigalle

Getting better all the time

The 9th arrondissement was where horse-drawn carriages would deliver aristocrats to the Palais Garnier; where men converged to witness the sultry high kicks of the cancan; where classic art lots went under the hammer at the Hôtel Drouot; and where the beating heart of "Gay Paree" could be found.

At the top of the arrondissement is the neighbourhood of South Pigalle. For decades this melting pot of classes was home to politicians, the art world's elite and their mistresses. Now the area acts as a meeting point for the city's young bohemians who come here for the live-music scene and restaurant culture.

The action in SoPi, as some now call it, mainly centres around Rue des Martyrs. This busy street was named after the martyrdom of Saint Denis in the 5th century who, legend has it, picked up his head after he was beheaded and walked for miles before eventually dying. It's home to a number of longstanding merchants, including the softly spoken gentleman at Fromagerie Chataigner, the gruff butcher at Aux Saveurs d'Auvergne, honey shop Famille Mary (open since 1921) and gourmet jam and condiment purveyor La Chambre aux Confitures. The newcomers have branched out into the surrounding side streets and are bringing a new energy to this bijou neighbourhood.

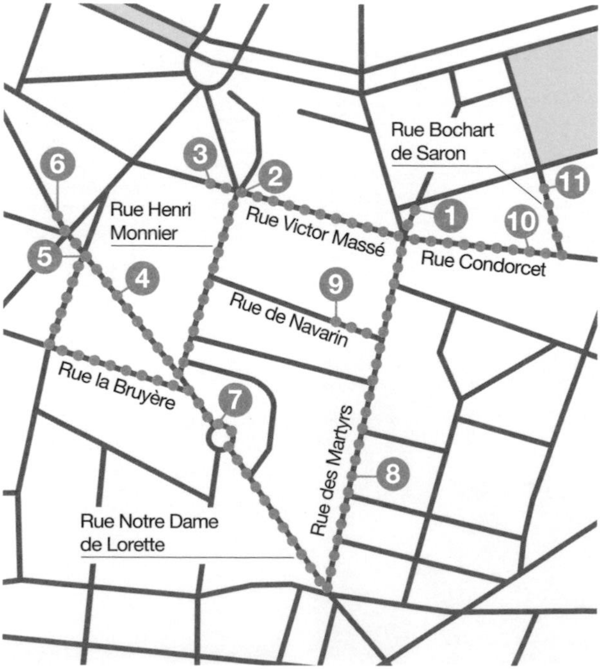

Hot spot

South Pigalle walk

The ❶ *KB Caféshop* is a good place to start the day with a fresh juice or coffee. Owner Nicolas Piégay honed his barista skills in Sydney and his staff serve a commendable flat white. Once finished, head down across the square and walk along Rue Victor Massé.

Notice the musical theme rippling through the street, with shops offering acoustic and electric guitars, percussion and even the occasional brass ensemble. Before crossing the street you'll spot the ❷ *Place Gabriel Kaspereit* gated community to your right. Late greats who called this cul-de-sac home include 19th-century poet Victor Hugo, film director Jean Renoir and painter Henri de Toulouse-Lautrec. Vincent van Gogh allegedly briefly squatted at his brother's apartment across the road at number 25.

On the other side of the intersection to your left is ❸ *Oldies Guitars*. Peruse the collection of vintage instruments then head back and turn down Rue Henri Monnier. You can pop into Buvette on your left for a glass of wine or continue on, rounding the corner to your right at the major intersection to head up Rue Notre-Dame de Lorette; stop in at ❹ *Sept Cinq*. Audrey Gallier and Lorna Moquet are behind this concept store with its collection of clothing, accessories and homeware designed in Paris.

Further up the street on the corner is the upmarket general store ❺ *Causses*, which stocks

Getting there

The Pigalle Metro station is serviced by Lines 2 and 12 and is a five-minute walk downhill to the starting point. Bus route 67, travelling from the south, also stops just outside the station.

organic food. The fertile land in the middle of France is the shop's namesake and there is also a homely bistro at the back where you can stop for a traditional lunch. If you are in the mood for something a little different, exit and head across the junction to ❻ *Ito Chan*, where bento boxes and ramen are on the lunch menu. Head back to the intersection and walk down Rue de la Rochefoucauld, passing the puntastic Sax Machine shop. Next turn left onto Rue la Bruyère and admire the greenery spilling from the balconies.

Take a right at the Fondation Taylor gallery, crossing the road to your right at ❼ *Place Saint-Georges*. Dating to 1824, the fountain in the centre was once a horse trough; the Bibliothèque Thiers building was the home of politician and historian Adolphe Thiers. Next continue to the end of Rue Notre-Dame de Lorette, veering to your left and taking another left up Rue des Martyrs, the heart of Pigalle. La Maison Seurre, one of the oldest residents on the street and indeed one of the oldest pâtisseries in the city, came under the ❽ *Sébastien Gaudard* banner in 2011. Gaudard renovated the now eponymous shop and bakes only the classics.

Ahead on the left is Rue de Navarin, where you'll spot the neon-pink sign and inconspicuous black doors of ❾ *Hôtel Amour*. The 20-room hotel is an ode to Pigalle's provocative past, where eroticism trumps romance when it comes to decor and the well-potted atrium attracts a steady stream of à la mode diners.

Walk back to Rue des Martyrs, take a left and then turn right down Rue Condorcet, stopping at vintage shop ❿ *Retro Chic*. Owner Yan Durand Lancien has been dealing in high-end and rare collections for years and opened his Pigalle shop in 2012.

To wind down the walk turn right out of Retro Chic, take a left onto Rue Bochart de Saron and pull up a stool at the elegant ⓫ *Artisan*. The cocktail menu is in constant rotation and seldom bows to haughty trends, serving classics informed by seasonal produce.

Address book

01 KB Caféshop
53 Avenue Trudaine, 75009
+33 (0)1 5692 1241

02 Place Gabriel Kaspereit
Avenue Frochot, 75009

03 Oldies Guitars
31 Rue Victor Massé, 75009
+33 (0)1 4280 9366

04 Sept Cinq
54 Rue Notre-Dame de Lorette, 75009
+33 (0)9 8355 0595
sept-cinq.com

05 Causses
55 Rue Notre-Dame de Lorette, 75009
+33 (0)1 5316 1010
causses.org

06 Ito Chan
2 Rue Pierre Fontaine, 75009
+33 (0)9 5171 9544
itoeats.fr

07 Place Saint-Georges
Corner of Rue Saint-Georges and Rue Notre-Dame de Lorette, 75009

08 Sébastien Gaudard
22 Rue des Martyrs, 75009
+33 (0)1 7118 2470
sebastiengaudard.com

09 Hôtel Amour
8 Rue de Navarin, 75009
+33 (0)1 4878 3180
hotelamourparis.fr

10 Retro Chic
57 Rue Condorcet, 75009
+33 (0)6 1793 0364

11 Artisan
14 Rue Bochart de Saron, 75009
+33 (0)1 4874 6538
artisan-bar.fr

NEIGHBOURHOOD 04

Montmartre
Picture perfect

Perched on a hilltop in northern Paris, the snow-white domes of the Sacré-Coeur tower above the city. It's a monument that's impossible to miss and it's well worth a trek to the 18th arrondissement. But there's far more to Montmartre than its basilica. In the 19th and 20th centuries the neighbourhood, which is characterised by its charming cobbled streets and beautiful vistas, was home to the most important artists, singers and writers of their time, including Pablo Picasso, Édith Piaf and Émile Zola. Renoir immortalised the ambience of the district's bohemian days in his painting "Bal du moulin de la Galette", which depicts the street corner where Paris's two remaining windmills stand as a reminder of the rural village Montmartre used to be before it officially became part of the city in 1860.

Today the neighbourhood is bordered by Rue Caulaincourt to the northwest, Rue de Clignancourt to the east and boulevards Clichy and Rochechouart to the south. Here you'll find everything Paris is known for: art, history and romance. And while Montmartre's magic may have dissipated since its heyday, we'll show you the best paths to take to avoid the crowds and see this part of town as it's meant to be seen: as the neighbourhood that inspired legions of artists.

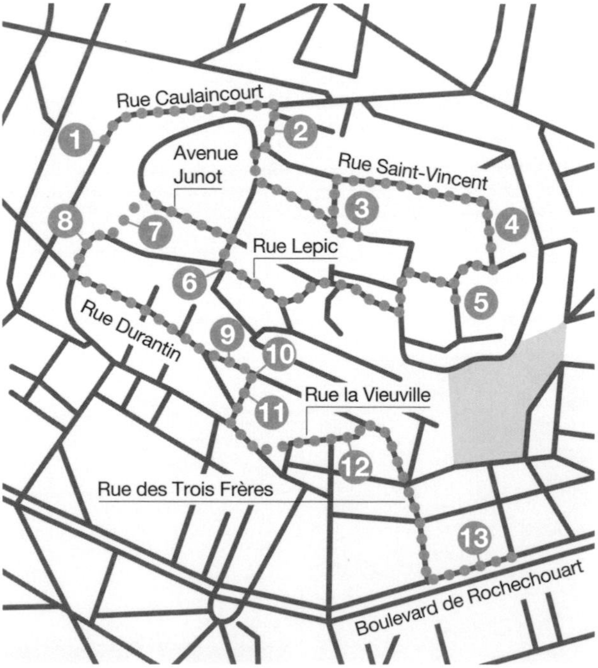

Art of the matter
Montmartre walk

Begin your walk at Lamarck-Caulaincourt. As you leave the station, turn away from the newspaper kiosk and make your way up the staircase that leads to Rue Caulaincourt. The only way to start the day in Paris is with a croissant, a cup of coffee and the morning paper; the best place is ❶ *Boris Lumé la pâtisserie*. To get there turn right at the top of the staircase and follow the street (and the smell of freshly baked baguettes) until you reach number 48.

Croissant in hand, double back until you reach the leafy Square Joël Le Tac. Along the left side of the square you'll come across the bookshop ❷ *L'Attrape-Coeurs*, where you can pick up a copy of Zola's *Germinal* (the novelist lived in the neighbourhood and now rests in Montmartre Cemetery) before you make your way up the stone staircase at the top of the square. Turn left onto Rue de l'Abreuvoir, which curves uphill and grants you a beautiful view of Sacré-Coeur's ivory towers. As you follow the street you'll come to Montmartre's oldest house at 12 Rue Cortot, which dates to the 17th century and is now home to the ❸ *Musée de Montmartre*. It recounts the history of the neighbourhood and in its garden you'll see the spot where Renoir painted "La Balançoire" ("The Swing") among other masterpieces.

After taking in some culture, head right onto Rue des Saules to find the city's last vineyard, which continues to yield about 1,500 bottles of gamay and pinot noir a year. Further downhill, at the corner to Rue Saint-Vincent, you'll see Au Lapin Agile, an authentic 19th-century cabaret. From here, keep right and meander along Rue Saint-Vincent until you reach 4 *Square Marcel Bleustein-Blanchet*, where you can join in a round of pétanque and from where you'll have a picture-perfect view of the back of 5 *Sacré-Coeur*. Stroll around the basilica and keep your eyes open for the Église Saint-Pierre de Montmartre: it's one of the city's oldest surviving churches, consecrated in 1147.

At this point you'll find the streets getting more crowded so pick up the

pace. Walk along Rue du Chevalier de la Barre, turn left onto Rue du Mont Cenis and then right onto Rue Norvins, where you'll hit the bustling Place du Tertre, dotted with stands hawking souvenirs and artists poised to sketch portraits of passers-by. At Place Jean-Baptise Clément turn left until you reach Rue Lepic, at which point you'll want to turn right and follow the road until you spot the city's last two windmills at 6 *Le Moulin de la Galette*.

From here, turn into Rue Girardon and then left onto Avenue Junot as you make your way to the 7 *Maison de Tristan Tzara*, home to a 20th-century poet and designed by renowned architect Adolf Loos. Then wander down Passage Com M18 back onto Rue Lepic, at the corner of which there's the lovely *épicerie* 8 *Jeanne B*. After a bite, turn left onto Rue Durantin and keep going until you reach 9 *Le Bateau-Lavoir* in Place Émile-Goudeau. It was here that Picasso painted "Les Demoiselles d'Avignon" in 1907. Head down the hill past pâtisserie 10 *Gilles Marchal* and don't forget to stop at 11 *Café Tabac* for some homemade treats and freshly brewed Genovese coffee.

After a pick-me-up, head down to Rue des Abbesses and walk past the Wall of Love (inscribed with "I love you" in 250 languages) in Square Rictus until you reach Rue la Vieuville. Drop in at concept store 12 *Spree*, then make your way down Rue des Trois Frères until you reach the famous concert hall 13 *Le Trianon* on Boulevard de Rochechouart. Just across the road there's the Anvers Metro station, which will take you home after you've had your fill of live music for the day.

Getting there

Jump on Line 12 and get off at Lamarck-Caulaincourt. On the way back, get on Line 2 (blue) at Anvers, which will take you all the way to Charles de Gaulle Étoile, where you'll find the Arc de Triomphe.

Address book

01 Boris Lumé la pâtisserie
48 Rue Caulaincourt, 75018

02 L'Attrape-Coeurs
4 Place Constantin Pecqueur, 75018
+33 (0)1 4252 0561

03 Musée de Montmartre
12-14 Rue Cortot, 75018
+33 (0)1 4925 8939
museedemontmartre.fr

04 Square Marcel Bleustein-Blanchet
Rue de la Bonne, 75018
equipement.paris.fr

05 Sacré-Coeur
35 Rue du Chevalier de la Barre, 75018
sacre-coeur-montmartre.com

06 Le Moulin de la Galette
83 Rue Lepic, 75018
+33 (0)1 4606 8477
lemoulindelagalette.fr

07 Maison de Tristan Tzara
15 Avenue Junot, 75018

08 Jeanne B
61 Rue Lepic, 75018
+33 (0)1 4251 1753
jeanne-b-comestibles.com

09 Le Bateau-Lavoir
13 Place Émile-Goudeau, 75018

10 Gilles Marchal
9 Rue Ravignan, 75018
+33 (0)1 8534 7330
gillesmarchal.com

11 Café Tabac
1 Rue Ravignan, 75018
+33 (0)1 4251 4453

12 Spree
16 Rue la Vieuville, 75018
spree.fr

13 Le Trianon
80 Boulevard de Rochechouart, 75018
letrianon.fr

NEIGHBOURHOOD 05

Saint-Germain-des-Prés
Seine-side sights

While this Left Bank suburb is now one of the city's swankiest districts, it was historically the epicentre of Paris's art and intellectual community. During the 19th century the likes of Balzac and Manet would hold court in its cafés; after the Second World War, Sartre, Simone de Beauvoir, Beckett and Picasso famously whiled away their days and nights debating and carousing in its gritty bistros and coffee houses.

Today their old haunts, such as Café de Flore and Les Deux Magots, are filled to the brim with tourists and the streets are lined with high-end boutiques and restaurants. But the area still retains its links to its arty beginnings through the galleries and art dealers who call it home. The main artery running through the neighbourhood, Boulevard Saint-Germain, was one of the new streets that transformed the city in the 19th century under Haussmann. While no visit would be complete without viewing its magnificent buildings from this era, we recommend wandering through the backstreets and secret passageways as well.

Among the shops selling tat for tourists you'll discover tranquil gardens and squares along with exceptional museums and art galleries, plus places where you can walk in the footsteps of some of the city's most famous sons and daughters. Top it all off with a Seine-side picnic and you really will be getting a slice of Parisian culture.

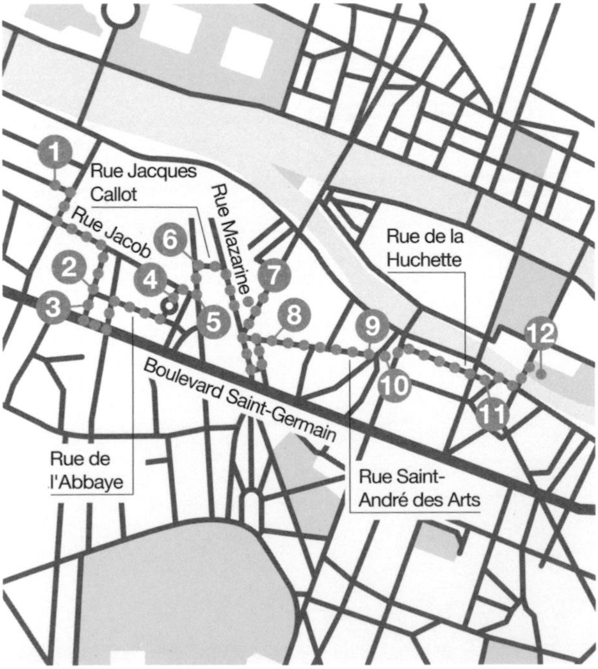

See and be seen
Saint-Germain-des-Prés walk

Start your walk from ❶ *La Maison de Serge Gainsbourg*, the graffiti-covered former home of the city's most famous Lothario and arts figure. It bears messages of love from fans and an ever-changing tableau of street art. If you're facing the house, turn left and walk to Rue des Saints-Pères and turn right. Take the first left onto Rue Jacob and then after one block turn right onto Rue Saint-Benoît. You'll soon come to ❷ *Le Chocolat Alain Ducasse*; don't miss sampling the chef's famous pralines. Just next door you'll see the green-and-white awning of the iconic ❸ *Café de Flore*. Stop for a coffee and pretend you're back in the days when Pablo Picasso and Georges Bataille were regulars.

Exit and turn left on Boulevard Saint-Germain, then take the first left onto Place Saint-Germain-des-Prés and the first right onto Rue de l'Abbaye. You'll pass the Abbey of Saint-Germain-des-Prés, the landmark that gave this area its name. Descartes is buried in one of its side chapels.

When you hit Rue de Furstenberg, turn left and pass through the charming Place Furstenberg. At number 6 you'll come to ❹ *Musée National Eugène Delacroix*, the former studio and home of the famous painter. It's small but filled with interesting artworks and there is a lovely garden. Exit and continue until you hit Rue Jacob again. Turn right and cross Rue de l'Echaudé. ❺ *Boutique Isabel Marant* is on your right-hand side and is a great place for fashion-forward designs for women.

By now you're probably in need of something to eat. Walk north on Rue de Seine until you hit 6 *La Palette*. Its terrace is a lovely place for a meal. Exit and walk back to Rue Jacques Callot and turn left. Turn right at Rue Mazarine and left down the pretty Passage Dauphine. After emerging, turn left to visit 7 *Librairie Couleur du Temps*, a bookshop specialising in design, art and fashion titles.

Exit and head back south on Rue Dauphine, continuing when it turns into Rue de l'Ancienne-Comédie. When you are almost at the intersection of Boulevard Saint-Germain, look for a passageway on your left called Cours du Commerce Saint-André. This quaint walkway is lined with boutiques and cafés, including the city's oldest coffee shop, Le Procope, which opened in 1686.

Continue and exit onto Rue Saint-André des Arts and turn right. Look out for 8 *Galerie Kamel Mennour* (*see page 100*), one of the city's leading galleries for both up-and-coming and established artists. Continue until you reach Boulevard Saint-Michel and cross to see 9 *Fontaine Saint-Michel*, the water feature commissioned by Haussmann that depicts the archangel Michael defeating the devil. Continue across the road to admire art nouveau 10 *Saint-Michel Metro station*, designed by Hector Guimard (*see pages 120 &121*).

Head down the busy Rue de la Huchette. Don't let the crowds of tourists and the takeaway shops deter you. Cross Rue du Petit Pont onto Rue de la Bûcherie. On your right you'll see 11 *Shakespeare and Company*, one of the world's most renowned bookshops (*see page 61*). Hours can be spent browsing its labyrinthine interiors and the café is a good spot for a break. When you're done, continue until you reach Rue Saint-Julien le Pauvre. Turn left and then right again when you hit the river. At the first bridge cross for a view of 12 *Notre-Dame Cathedral*, the city's Gothic masterpiece. For a better view of the flying buttresses and gargoyles, walk to the right and enter Square Jean XXIII. This pretty park also offers plenty of shaded seating to cool your heels after your explorations.

Getting there

The Saint-Germain-des-Prés station is a stop on Line 4, which travels through the heart of Paris. Exit the station on Boulevard Saint-Germain then walk north towards the Seine to make your way to Rue de Verneuil – and the start of the walk.

Address book

01 La Maison de Serge Gainsbourg
5 Rue de Verneuil, 75006

02 Le Chocolat Alain Ducasse
26 Rue Saint-Benoît, 75006
+33 (0)1 4548 8789
lechocolat-alainducasse.com

03 Café de Flore
172 Boulevard Saint-Germain, 75006
+33 (0)1 4548 5526

04 Musée National Eugène Delacroix
6 Rue de Furstenberg, 75006
+33 (0)1 4441 8650
musee-delacroix.fr

05 Boutique Isabel Marant
1 Rue Jacob, 75006
+33 (0)1 4326 0412
isabelmarant.com

06 La Palette
43 Rue de Seine, 75006
+33 (0)1 4326 6815
cafelapaletteparis.com

07 Librairie Couleur du Temps
24 Rue Dauphine, 75006
+33 (0)1 4325 6916
librairie-couleurdutemps.com

08 Galerie Kamel Mennour
47 Rue Saint-André des Arts, 75006
+33 (0)1 5624 0363
kamelmennour.com

09 Fontaine Saint-Michel
Place Saint-Michel, 75006

10 Saint-Michel Metro station
Boulevard Saint-Michel

11 Shakespeare and Company
37 Rue de la Bûcherie, 75005
+33 (0)1 4325 4093
shakespeareandcompany.com

12 Notre-Dame Cathedral
6 Place du Parvis Notre-Dame, 75004
+33 (0)1 4234 5610
cathedraledeparis.com

Resources
—— Inside knowledge

So now you know about the boutiques, bakeries, gastronomic gems and galleries. Given Paris's easy walkability and its excellent public-bike scheme, we suggest getting around above ground to get to them when you can. The circuitous streets can be tricky to navigate but getting lost in pretty passages is half the fun. Alternatively, the metro system is relatively straightforward.

We've also listed the slang you'll overhear (and perhaps use if you want to try to blend in), a soundtrack to inspire and colour your explorations plus all-weather activities to see you through come rain or shine.

You'll spend plenty of time dodging smokers and scooters but trust us: you'll also find plenty of singular little moments to savour in this city.

Transport
Get around town

01 **Metro:** Remember quaint paper tickets? The French still use them on the Metro. They can be purchased for one, two, three or five-day periods of unlimited use or as single-use (€1.80). Special tickets to the airports cost €7.70 each way. *ratp.fr*

02 **Bus:** Travel by bus can be slow. Buses are often filled with baby carriages as they are the preferred transport of parents with young children (the Metro has few escalators). Note that tickets between Metro and bus rides are non-transferable. *ratp.fr*

03 **Vélib':** The public-bike scheme is beloved by visitors and locals alike. Journeys of 30 minutes or less are free; usage charges apply if you exceed this (the first extra half an hour is €1 but this quickly escalates). If you're an avid cycler it's worth buying a 24-hour ticket (€1.70). Download the app to find stations. *velib.paris.fr*

04 **Boat:** The shuttle boats offer peaceful sightseeing (they glide past Musée du Louvre, Eiffel Tower and Notre Dame Cathedral). A day pass is €16. *batobus.com*

05 **On foot:** Paris is very walkable. Those who get disoriented can consult the maps on the side of public toilets but keep an eye on the ground to avoid dog excrement; despite some improvement, many Parisians are still lax about picking it up.

06 **Taxi and private car:** Taxis can be a little scarce when you want to hail one, except in central areas and near stations. Once inside there is a service charge and the rates are based on zone and time.

07 **Flights:** Charles de Gaulle Airport is 25km north of the city and Orly Aiport is 18km to the south. Both are accessible by the RER B. *ratp.fr*

Vocabulary
Local lingo

French people are always saying things *au second degré* – with irony – but here are some common terms.

01 **A ta santé:** To your health (cheers)
02 **Balle:** Quid/buck
03 **Bises/bisous:** Kisses
04 **Fumer une clope:** Have a smoke
05 **L'addition:** The bill
06 **Salut:** Hi or bye

Soundtrack to the city
Top tunes

01 **Yves Montand, 'Les Grands Boulevards':** *"J'aime flâner sur les grands boulevards"* — "I like to stroll on the boulevards" — is pretty much the city's mantra.

02 **Jacques Dutronc, 'Il Est Cinq Heures Paris S'Éveille':** A song celebrating that overlap when late-nighters power down and early-morning businesses start up.

03 **Ladyhawke, 'Paris is Burning':** She may be a Kiwi but Phillipa Brown captures the frenetic energy of going out drinking in the French capital.

04 **Friendly Fires, 'Paris (Aeroplane Remix)':** Because at one stage we've all said to ourselves: "One day I'm gonna live in Paris."

05 **Jonathan Richman and the Modern Lovers, 'Give Paris One More Chance':** Richman invokes the legacies of great French *chanteurs* and *chanteuses* (Aznavour, Piaf, Trenet) and champions the City of Love to non-believers.

06 **Jane Birkin and Serge Gainsbourg, 'Je T'aime... Moi Non Plus'** Gainsbourg originally recorded this sexy song with Brigitte Bardot but it was shelved when her husband kicked up a fuss. Jane Birkin stepped in and it became a classic.

Best events
What to see

01 **Omnivore:** A series of masterclasses, pop-up dinners and culinary events by established and up-and-coming chefs.
March, omnivore.com

02 **Paris Beer Week:** A nod to the nascent craft-beer scene.
April-May, laparisbeer week.com

03 **Monumenta:** A biannual large-scale installation by a major contemporary artist, under the Nave of the Grand Palais.
May-June, grandpalais.fr

04 **Roland Garros:** Held over three weeks at the stadium named after the French aviator, this is the only clay-court grand-slam event.
May-June, rolandgarros.com

05 **Cinéma en Plein Air:** Free outdoor screenings, during which the whole of Paris gathers for movies and outdoor picnicking.
July-August, lavillette.com/evenement/cinema-en-plein-air-home-cinema

06 **Maison et Objet:** A biannual design trade fair.
January & September, maison-objet.com

07 **Jazz à la Villette:** The musical line-up transitions the city from lazy late summer into active early autumn.
September, jazzalavillette.com

08 **FIAC:** A blockbuster international art fair, with installations peppered throughout the city.
October, fiac.com/paris

09 **Pitchfork Paris:** Cool bands from the US and the UK gathered under the lofty roof of the Grande Halle de La Villette.
October, pitchforkmusic festival.fr

10 **Paris Photo:** An international selection of galleries within the photography world, with ambitious and impressive scope.
November, parisphoto.com

Rainy days
Weather-proof activities

Parisians do not handle rain very well. Luckily there is a wealth of indoor attractions and museums to explore when it's wet out.

01 **Rue des Écoles:** Several cinema houses stud the Rue des Écoles. These venues regularly show director retrospectives and classics from American, French, Italian, and Asian repertoires. Curl up in one of the small, cosy theatres; in this capital of cinephiles, the quality and quantity of screenings on offer is beyond compare.
lechampo.com
lafilmotheque.fr
legrandaction.com

02 **Explore a museum:** On a grim day, the riches of Paris's extensive collection of museums provide wondrous respite. For intimate viewing without the crowds try a smaller museum such as the Musée National Gustave Moreau or the Fondation Henri Cartier-Bresson. Other tranquil spots are the recently reopened Musée de l'Homme (for anthropological marvels) and the transport-design treasures of the Musée des Arts et Métiers.

03 **Go shopping:** Poke around the covered passageways and marvel at the centuries-old arcades at the threshold between the 2nd and 9th arrondissements. Passage des Panoramas was built in 1800 and is the oldest remaining structure; it's home to stamp sellers, collectibles at Tombées du Camion, a gluten-free café and wine bars. Galerie Vivienne, built in 1823, has elaborate mosaic floors, an Alexis Mabille boutique, a watchmaker's shop and wines at Le Bougainville. In the 1846 Passage Jouffroy you'll find lovely toy- and bookshops – and be sure to take a look at the heritage-listed Hôtel Chopin.

Sunny days
The great outdoors

When the sun is shining the French capital is nothing less than magic. Here are three ways to soak it up.

01 **Parc de la Villette:** Originally built as an abattoir under Haussmann in 1858, today this place is a beast-free, flat and walkable space with green stretches and bright-red structures by architect Bernard Tschumi. Check out the oversized bicycle-wheel statue by Claes Oldenburg and wander past the reflective sci-fi wonder of the Géode. Also nearby are the Cité des Sciences, several music venues such as the Cabaret Sauvage and le Trabendo and the shimmering Jean Nouvel-designed Philharmonie de Paris.
lavillette.com

02 **High-line park:** This tree-lined beltway atop the former Vincennes railway line – defunct since the late 1960s – spans 4.7km of pedestrian-only strolling (with some dedicated cyclist access). Designed by landscape architect Jacques Vergely and architect Philippe Mathieux, its path meanders east to the edge of the city ring. Inaugurated in 1993, it was the only elevated park until New York's High Line was unveiled in 2009.

03 **Picnic on the river:** You'll be hard-pressed to find a spot for yourself along the riverbank when the sun is shining and Parisians come out to picnic but squeeze in as best you can – and bring along some wine and tasty accoutrements. To start the conversation with neighbouring picnickers, ask to borrow their bottle opener. Our favourite spots are along the Quai de Jemmapes or Quai de Vamy in the 10th arrondissement or in the public space near Notre Dame Cathedral.

About Monocle
—— Step inside

In 2007, Monocle was launched as a monthly magazine briefing on global affairs, business, culture, design and much more. We believed there was a globally minded audience of readers who were hungry for opportunities and experiences beyond their national borders.

Today Monocle is a complete media brand with print, audio and online elements – not to mention our expanding retail network and online business. Besides our London HQ we have six international bureaux in New York, Toronto, Singapore, Tokyo, Zürich and Hong Kong. We continue to grow and flourish and at our core is the simple belief that there will always be a place for a print brand that is committed to telling fresh stories and sending photographers on assignments. It's also a case of knowing that our success is all down to the readers, advertisers and collaborators who have supported us along the way.

1

International bureaux
Boots on the ground

We have an HQ in London and call upon firsthand reports from our contributors in more than 35 cities around the world. We also have six international bureaux; for this travel guide, editor Amy Richardson hopped over the channel to immerse herself in the French capital, helped out by Mikaela Aitken and our Paris-based fashion director Daphné Hézard. They also called on the assistance of writers in the city to ensure we have covered the best food, retail, hospitality and entertainment on offer. The aim is to make you, the reader, feel like a local when you visit.

In the know
—
French fashion director Daphné Hézard

On air
—
Our radio studios are on site at Midori House

2
Radio
Sound approach

Monocle 24 is our round-the-clock radio station that was launched in 2011. It delivers global news and shows covering foreign affairs, urbanism, business, culture, food and drink, design and print media. When you find yourself in Paris you can listen to *The Globalist*, our morning news programme that is the perfect way to start the day in Europe; Monocle 24's editors, presenters and guests set the agenda in international news and business. We also have a playlist to accompany you day and night, regularly assisted by live sessions that are hosted at our Midori House headquarters.

3
Print
Committed to the page

MONOCLE is published 10 times a year. We have stayed loyal to our belief in quality print with two new seasonal publications: THE FORECAST, packed with key insights into the year ahead, and THE ESCAPIST, our summer travel-minded magazine. To sign up visit *monocle.com/subscribe*. Since 2013 we have also been publishing books, like this one, in partnership with Gestalten.

4
Online
Digital delivery

We also have a dynamic website: *monocle.com*. As well as being the place to hear Monocle 24, we use the site to present our films, which are beautifully shot and edited by our in-house team and provide a fresh perspective on our stories. Check out the films celebrating the cities that make up our Travel Guide Series before you explore the rest of the site.

5
Retail and cafés
Good taste

Via our shops in Hong Kong, Toronto, New York, Tokyo, London and Singapore we sell products that cater to our readers' tastes and are produced in collaboration with brands we believe in. We also have cafés in Tokyo and London serving coffee and Japanese delicacies among other things – and we are set to expand this arm of our business.

Join us

There are lots of ways to be part of the ever-expanding monocle world whether in print, online, or on your radio. We'd love to have you join the club.

01 Read the magazine

You can buy monocle magazine at newsstands in more than 60 countries around the world, or get yourself an annual subscription at *monocle.com.*

02 Listen to Monocle 24

You can tune in to Monocle 24 radio live via our free app, at *monocle.com* or on any internet-enabled radio. Or download our shows from iTunes or SoundCloud to keep informed as you travel the globe.

03 Subscribe to the Monocle Minute

Sign up today to the Monocle Minute, our free daily news and views email, at *monocle.com*. Our website is also where you'll find a world of free films, our online shop and updates about everything that we are up to.

MONOCLE

Keeping an eye and an ear on the world

Writers
Mikaela Aitken
Margault Antonini
Chloë Ashby
Kathy Ball
Tom Burges Watson
Melkon Charchoglyan
Philippe Cohen Solal
Eugenia Ellanskaya
Raphaël Fejtö
Ines Fressynet
Daphné Hézard
Aidan McLaughlin
Sarah Moroz
David Plaisant
Amy Richardson
Marie-Sophie Schwarzer
Heather Stimmler-Hall
Sonia Zhuravlyova

Chief photographer
François Cavelier

Still life
David Sykes

Photographers
Aurélien Bergot
Alex Cretey Systermans
Thomas Humery
Fred Lahache
Renaud Marion
Lola Reboud
Yoann Stoeckel

Images
Michael Adelo
Alamy
Francis Amiand
Arnaud André
Martin Argyroglo
Andrea Aversa
Thomas Balaÿ
Guillaume Belvèze
Patrick Berger
Martin Bidou
Karen Blumberg
Luc Boegly
Nicolas Borel
David Boureau
Burgermac
Nicholas Calcott
Christophe Caudroy
Adrien Chevrot
François Coquerel
Alban Couturier
Floriane de Lassée
Pascal Dhennequin
Marc Domage
Charles Duprat
Rebecca Fanuele
Fatina Faye
Barbara Feichtinger
Georges Fessy
Daniele Fherm
François Flohic
Edouard François
Philippe Garcia
Virginie Garnier
Tim Geraghty-Groves
Getty Images
Christophe Glaudel
Hervé Goluza
Fabrice Gousset
Guillaume Grasset
Alexandre Guirkinger
Karl Hab
Thomas Humery
iStock
Nicolas Jacquemin
Julie Joubert
Stephen Kent Johnson
Kristof Kicherer
Hervé Lewandowski
Pascal Martinez
Douglas McWall
Di Messina
Aurélien Mole
Teddy Morellec
Emmanuel Naxos
Bernard Nicolau-Bergeret
Jean-Philippe Baltel
Olivier Placet
Philippe Pumain
Paul Raftery
Cyrille Robin
Philippe Ruault
Julian Salinas
Chiara Santarelli
Philippe Servent
Thai Toutain
Robert Valerio
Bernhard Winkelmann
Guillaume Ziccarelli

Illustrators
Satoshi Hashimoto
Tokuma
Don Mak

Monocle
EDITOR IN CHIEF AND CHAIRMAN
Tyler Brûlé
EDITOR
Andrew Tuck
CREATIVE DIRECTOR
Richard Spencer Powell

The Monocle Travel Guide Series: Paris
GUIDE EDITOR
Amy Richardson
ASSOCIATE GUIDE EDITOR
Daphné Hézard
PHOTO EDITORS
Renee Melides
Shin Miura
Poppy Shibamoto
Victoria Cagol
DESIGNERS
Kate McInerney
Jay Yeo
Sam Brogan
Loi Xuan Ly

The Monocle Travel Guide Series
SERIES EDITOR
Joe Pickard
ASSOCIATE EDITOR
Chloë Ashby
ASSISTANT EDITOR
Mikaela Aitken
RESEARCHER
Melkon Charchoglyan
DESIGNER
Loi Xuan Ly
PHOTO EDITORS
Matthew Beaman
Victoria Cagol
Shin Miura

PRODUCTION
Jacqueline Deacon
Dan Poole
Rachel Kurzfield
Sean McGeady
Sonia Zhuravlyova

CHAPTER EDITING

Need to know
Sarah Moroz

H 1
Hotels
Amy Richardson

F 2
Food and drink
Amy Richardson

R 3
Retail
Daphné Hézard

T 4
Things we'd buy
Daphné Hézard

E 5
Essays
Amy Richardson

C 6
Culture
Amy Richardson

D 7
Design and architecture
David Plaisant

S 8
Sport and fitness
David Plaisant

W 9
Walks
David Plaisant

Resources
Sarah Moroz

Research
Mikaela Aitken
Margault Antonini
Melkon Charchoglyan
Eugénie Derez
Eugenia Ellanskaya
Ines Fressynet
Daphné Hézard
Ilana Hanukov
Aidan McLaughlin
Sarah Moroz
Marie-Sophie Schwarzer
Alexandra Stapleton

Special thanks
Kathy Ball
Paul Fairclough
Lee Gale
Ed Lawrenson
Andrew Urwin

New

The collection

Planning another trip? We have a global suite of guides, with many more set to be released in the coming months. Cities are fun. Let's explore.

Buy today at all good bookshops

You can also visit the online shops at *monocle.com* and *shop.gestalten.com* to get hold of your copies.

1. London
2. New York
3. Tokyo
4. Hong Kong
5. Madrid
6. Bangkok
7. Istanbul
8. Miami
9. Rio de Janeiro
10. Paris
11. Singapore
12. Vienna
13. Sydney
14. Honolulu
15. Copenhagen
16. Los Angeles
17. Toronto
18. Berlin
19. Rome
20. Venice
21. Amsterdam
22. Stockholm
23. Lisbon
24. Munich
25. Milan
26. San Francisco
27. Kyoto